Trish Griffin was born and bred in outback Queensland on a large sheep and cattle station during the 1950's. The isolation and freedom of her childhood gave birth to an overwhelming desire to explore the world. She followed this urge with great passion, usually travelling the hard way—hitchhiking, local transport, horseback and more recently on foot.

Writing and literature have always been a passion for Trish, but she has never been tempted to write fiction, because she finds real life events and people far more interesting and unbelievable than any fiction.

Trish now lives in the beautiful seaside town of Kiama on the NSW coast, surrounded by ocean, mountains and grandchildren, her sources of inspiration.

Dancing on the Head of a Pin

Reflections on the Camino

AIA PUBLISHING

Trish Griffin

Dancing on the Head of a Pin: Reflections on the Camino
Trish Griffin
Copyright © 2020
Published by AIA Publishing, Australia
ABN: 32736122056
http://www.aiapublishing.com

All rights reserved. No part of this publication may be reproduced, stored in a retrieval system or transmitted in any form or by any means electronic, mechanical, audio, visual or otherwise, without prior permission of the copyright owner. Nor can it be circulated in any form of binding or cover other than that in which it is published and without similar conditions including this condition being imposed on the subsequent purchaser.

Paperback ISBN: 978-1-922329-05-9

Cover design by K. Rose Kreative

Gold texture used under a Creative Commons attributions licence from: www.textures4photoshop.com

I dedicate this book to:

Madeline, the inspiration for this journey.
The nuns, brothers and priests who persevered against the influence of my untamed childhood to instill the glories we have inherited from Western Civilization.
My secular-pilgrim companions that modified my sacred speculations.
My religious-pilgrim companions that modified my secular speculations.
The numerous angels that came to my rescue, constantly.
Most importantly, I would like to thank the people of Spain for protecting and nurturing their rich culture and heritage for well over two thousand years and preserving it for future generations.
Their dedication to this project is breath taking.

A Note on the Title and Cover

The question of how many angels can dance on the head of a pin is a *reductio ad absurdum* challenge posed to medieval religious scholasticism, an idea that has been discussed by Thomas Aquinas, George Bernard Shaw and other notable writers. I'm not suggesting I'm an angel with this title, only that so often during this journey, I felt little solid ground under my feet.

The image on the cover is the *Via Crucis* (Stations of the Cross) signal located inside the Cathedral in Santiago and is one of the oldest and significant artefacts on display. The two letters on the bottom, Alpha and Omega, are the first and last symbols of the Greek alphabet. The sun and moon stand for the merging of opposites, of unity and collaboration instead of conflict and strife.

Disclaimer

I have written this book over a period of eight years, so I've had to rely heavily on my memory. I didn't take notes on the journey as it was yet another thing to carry in my backpack. If there are any discrepancies, I apologize. Most of the characters have given me permission to use their names, but some asked to stay incognito.

Contents

Introduction	1
1. The Author	5
2. Madeline (Maddy)	9
3. Barcelona	13
4. Montserrat	19
5. Camino Catalan.	25
6. The Road to Pamplona	31
7. The Lurking Menace Strikes Again	37
8. Jaca	41
9. Sanguesa	45
10. Pamplona	49
11. Scientists, Spanish Grandmothers, & Other Useful Angels	55
12. Logrono	59
13. As Pants the Hart for Cooling Streams	63
14. Leon	67
15. Daily Departures Into the Realm of Shells & Arrows	73
16. Hospital da Orbigo	79
17. Ponferrada	85
18. Galica in all her Glory	91
19. Sarria	97
20. Monte de Guzo	101
21. Santiago: The Pilgrims' Mass	105
22. Passport to Nowhere	109
A Diabetic Perspective	113
Epilogue	117
A Note From the Author	121
Acknowledgements	123

Introduction

'It is a foolish thing to make a long prologue, and to be short in the story itself.' Maccabees, 11.

What am I doing here? Once again I asked myself the question often asked by misadventurers who've pushed the boundaries too far. This time I found myself at the top of a mountain trail in one of the remotest parts of Spain, suffering from a life-threatening hypoglycaemic episode. I'd consumed my last portion of glucose and there wasn't a soul in sight! That was only one of such moments.

In May 2012, after a stint of working two jobs nursing in Sydney for six months, I felt that I needed a good holiday. A close friend, Madeline (Maddy), invited me to join her on a pilgrimage in Spain, walking the Camino de Santiago de Compostela also known as the Way of St James. Maddy had already done four Caminos, had raved on about every one of them and previously asked me to join her. Usually I'd been tied down with work or family commitments, but when this opportunity arose, I found myself unencumbered. The idea of walking in Spain hadn't grabbed me because I'd often walked, cycled and ridden horses over the kind of hot, dry country we Australians have in abundance. I preferred to focus my travels around Alpine areas that fed my need for steep mountains, cool crisp air and spectacular scenery. Such cold places always had low populations and very few tourists. The thought of walking the latter part of this pilgrimage on busy trails did nothing to entice me. But Maddy piqued my curiosity by sending me photos she'd taken over the years displaying wondrous architecture and significant historical places.

And so I found myself on day one following the shells and arrows painted on posts, walls, streets, rocks, trees and so on that pointed the way to Montserrat Monastery. I quickly became completely immersed in my surroundings and discovered that I'd been locked into the Alpine pursuit for long enough. It was time to test the water with an utterly opposite venture.

Maddy chose for us to do two Caminos back to back, starting in Barcelona on the Camino Catalan and meeting up with the Camino Français, just north of Pamplona. Maddy's father had been born in the Costa Brava, not far north of Barcelona, and her heritage beckoned her to this region. Her objective was to walk from the Mediterranean to the Atlantic sea, 1300 kilometers in the space of forty-three days.

This pilgrimage started 1,200 years ago, some say well before, suggesting 5000 years. The early Celts used the trail a long time before Santiago existed. Their sages were said to have walked that path in the search for the occult knowledge of alchemy. There are too many Caminos to count, starting in far-flung places like Scandinavia, Scotland and Russia, but they all end in Santiago. The most popular and famous is the French route. The journey starts in France at St. Jean Pied de Port and finishes in the Cathedral of Santiago de Compostela in Galicia, Spain—a distance of 790 kilometers. In the Cathedral lies the shrine of St. James the apostle. Martyred in the holy land by King Herod Agrippa, his body was brought back to Santiago after the boat had been wrecked at sea and washed up on the shore covered with scallop shells. This is why the scallop shell is used to guide pilgrims on their journey. St. James is depicted in two contradictory ways: sometimes as a humble pilgrim in a big hat with staff in hand; other times as a warrior on horseback defeating the Moors with his lance. Maybe this iconography is a medieval representation of someone suffering from bipolar disorder!

Between the 8th and 12th century, this pilgrimage reached its zenith. It then went into decline until the late 20th century. In modern times, however, its popularity has been resurrected with an estimated 260,000 pilgrims finishing the Camino every year. The course remains unchanged since medieval times. It's supposed to follow the Ley Lines—lines of energy—that are believed by some to intersect at various places on the route. I chose not to explore the more esoteric components of this journey. I knew I had my work cut out just surviving the physical challenges. Today we cross the same bridges, pass through the same villages and quite often sleep in the same Refugio's and albergues—hostels designated to pilgrims.

Not everyone is suited to the Camino. Dealing—on a daily basis—with constant changes in weather, terrain, companionship, conflicts, physical pain and uncertainties about accommodation can cause a lot of discomfort. One enters a time warp, walking in the mindset of medieval Europe at a medieval pace. Some of the small villages remain largely unchanged since the 12th century, yet are only walking distance from modern bustling cities. This journey is like living in a functional museum, where history is alive, engaging, vibrant and dynamic—not locked away and rotting behind dusty glass cages. One day would find us watching a medieval jousting festival, another, joining locals in a religious procession honoring a long-gone saint or the occurrence of a miracle. The strength of the Spanish culture is wondrous. They are unashamedly proud and almost zealous about their history, which is ingrained into the whole calendar year; not a week passes without some community event. The Moorish occupation had such a big impact on Spain that re-enactments of famous battles are staged regularly everywhere, celebrating the victory of Ferdinand and Isabella, Charles Martel and El Cid. The entire village or city becomes involved in these re-enactments, from infants, all the way up to the stooped and aged.

The motives for doing this pilgrimage are as varied as the stars in the Compostela— such things as a holiday, an adventure, weight loss, divorce, death, illness and romance or lack thereof. Most pilgrims are seeking transformation of some sort, and most do not go home disappointed. The Camino de Santiago de Compostela is the classic Hero's Journey where one leaves the comforts and security of home to venture into the unknown, returning transformed and triumphant.

I didn't have any expectations, at least not consciously. At that stage of my life, I'd decided that my desires were unattainable and my many indiscretions, shortcomings and transgressions had been paid for ten times over. I was too cynical to believe that a long walk would be anything other than enjoyable and challenging. I felt full of unbridled optimism. My self-belief had me convinced that I was bomb proof and could rise above anything that the universe chose to throw my way—in physical terms at least.

The seven weeks of the pilgrimage severely tested this cockiness, leaving my feeling of invulnerability lying in shards along the Way. So often I was brought to my knees—physically, emotionally and spiritually. Arrogance was only one of the many unnecessary spiritual burdens with which I parted company.

They say that if you walk this path with an open heart and open mind, you can expect incredible shifts in consciousness. The Camino delivered so far beyond anything I could have expected. I'll try to convey to you the amazing experiences that came to me, unexpected and uninvited.

1. The Author

'If the fire in your heart is strong enough, it will burn away any obstacles that come your way.' Suzy Kassem

To help the reader understand why I struggled so much on this journey, I'll set out my background, particularly my medical history. I was fortunate enough to grow up on a remote cattle and sheep station in outback Queensland, Australia. As very young children, we ran wild and free, with very little restrictions, despite the hated hours we spent confined to the homestead classroom, learning through correspondence with the Mount Isa School of the Air. Children from outback stations are sent to boarding school on the coast at an early age, some as young as six. Though we hated the harsh environment of the schools, we learned to be resilient and independent. The school my parents chose was a Catholic convent in Brisbane, a French order strongly associated with the Jesuits. Their influence on our education was fortunate. Ahead of their time, they emphasized strength and independence in their girls and taught us to think beyond mere rationality. But their ascetic lifestyle was hard for kids living away from home.

Upon leaving school, a lot of us went nursing just to get away from the constraints of life in the bush. Back in the 1950s and 1960s, the opportunity for a university education was rarely an option for girls born into pastoral families. Woman were seen primarily as child bearers and were expected to marry into the appropriate families. I felt no different to the prize ewes and cows used for selective breeding. Pedigree was paramount.

Many of us fled. My fantasy as a seventeen-year old riding horses around in the red dust was to escape to an air-conditioned apartment in New York and attend cocktail parties in a black evening dress. I'd look so debonair with my long cigarette holder spilling ash over very expensive furnishings—a fantasy, probably brought on by reading *The Saturday Evening Post*. My mum lived in Townsville, North Queensland, during the Second World War. She, like most young women of the era, was infatuated with the American service men and culture. Many of our magazines, books and movies exuded America. The closest I got to New York, however, was Townsville—so much for my aspirations. Oh well, at least it rained there. After four years of nursing in Townsville—where I met Maddy—I went to Sydney, then the UK, Europe, and then to Thredbo in the Snowy Mountains of NSW, where I met my future husband, John.

John and I shared a passion for the wilderness and the sports that took us there—surfing, skiing, sailing, cross country running and, eventually, triathlon.

In 1987, at the age of thirty-eight, I reached the height of my athletic career. I qualified for the Australian Triathlon team to compete in the Hawaii Iron Man. I didn't know then that I was an undiagnosed insulin-dependent diabetic, even though I had the classic symptoms of extreme weight loss, constant thirst, leg cramps, and eventually blurred vision. You may think I must have been in a serious state of denial, but those symptoms were also signs of an athlete overtraining. The Iron Man course consists of a three-point-eight-kilometre swim, a 180 kilometre cycle, followed by a full Marathon of forty-two kilometres. To even make it to the starting line required being proficient in all three disciplines. To compete at the elite level required excellence in swimming, cycling and running. My training program was grueling, so when I demonstrated those symptoms, I merely thought I was preparing myself well for the challenge ahead.

Eventually, a concerned medical colleague suggested that I have a blood test. I was devastated to discover that my blood-sugar levels were so high that I could've gone into a coma! Needless to say, I was shocked, but perhaps I shouldn't have been that shocked since my family has a very strong history of diabetes, going back many generations—siblings, cousins, aunties, uncles, even my grandfather. We grew up with saucepans boiling away on the top of the stove, filled not with yummy treats but with glass syringes and needles. The medical specialist treated me with insulin. Unlike most other medications, insulin has to be delivered in just the right dosage. If the dose is too small, the high sugar levels (hyperglycaemia) can cause damage to the internal organs, eyes, kidneys, nerves and heart. If the dose is too large, there is a good chance that the blood-sugar levels will drop (hypoglycaemia), and if left untreated that will eventually result in loss of consciousness and death. I was told that I was a 'brittle diabetic' which reads as 'almost impossible to control' with enormous swings between high and low.

I found that using insulin was a bit like trying to peel an apple with a chain saw. I have survived numerous episodes of hypoglycemia, but there is always one waiting around the corner to take me out. After thirty-three years of battling this insidious monster with constant vigilance, I still cannot afford to treat it with contempt. I have sources of glucose on hand day and night.

Another hindrance on this journey—a much less serious impediment—was a broken bone in my foot that I'd sustained three months earlier. It hadn't healed properly because I had to continue my nursing commitments. I'd spent those months in a moon boot hobbling around the wards when I should've been training my body to walk long distances in the heat with a very heavy pack. Even so, I was pleasantly surprised when once I started walking, the bone only gave me a squeak here and there to remind me that it was less than happy.

With this story, I hope that others with this affliction will be able to gain some insight into their disease and gain the confidence required to take on similar challenges.

Sometimes I feel that I'm nudging up against the impossible just to keep body and soul together.

2. Madeline (Maddy)

'Don't walk behind me, I may not lead; don't walk in front of me, I may not follow; just walk beside me and be my friend.'
Albert Camus.

I would never have found myself on this journey if it wasn't for my long-standing friend, Maddy.

I remember when we first connected—over the water cooler outside ward 2B—as if it happened yesterday. On the first day of nursing training at a large teaching hospital in North Queensland, we were allocated to the same ward—a decision that the administration would come to rue! We had an instant connection while wilting under the tropical atmosphere in Townsville, relieved only by the biting chill of water from the cooler. The breeze blew hot and heavy, sweet with the fragrance of Frangipani, Coconut Palms and sea salt. The hospital, situated close to the sea with the briny breeze a constant, was our home for the next four years.

Our friendship was legend—at least during the four years we spent training. We shared everything from clothes, dates, shoes and pets to disciplinary actions and Honda motor scooters, but most of all we shared laughter. Young and reckless, we possessed virtually no inhibitions. In the late sixties, student nurses were kept under lock and key in quasi-military barracks called quarters for the duration of their four-year training. We had to be in bed with lights out by ten in the evening. Twice a week, a special pass allowed us to stay out until midnight. These restrictions were like waving a red rag in front of a bull for Maddy and I. The only rule we obeyed was the notion that rules are for fools. Our many great nights out were thanks to stuffing our beds with dummies and climbing through the back windows in the wee hours of the morning.

The supervisor eventually discovered the dummies with their wigs and evicted us from the Nursing Quarters. Thus began a new chapter of our relationship along with new-found freedoms. We lived in an old Queenslander on The Strand next to the Sea View Hotel, and before long other young women studying at university joined us.

In those days the wage for trainee nurses was the princely sum of twenty-eight dollars per fortnight. By day four we ran out of money. The only assets we had to hock were two unruly puppies that persisted in destroying everything in their path. We sold them to our neighbors for thirty dollars. That bought us a dinner at the local eatery—steak washed down with ubiquitous Cawarra Claret. Flush with good food and wine, we doubled on our Honda 50 back to the hospital in time for the night staff's midnight meal. On arrival, we rode up the ambulance ramp, into the lift and emerged in the dining room. There, much to the astonishment of all present, we rode our scooter around the tables until someone alerted us to the fact that the night supervisor was on her way, then we rode into the large cleaning cupboard and turned off the motor. I remember sitting there, my heart beating so loudly I was sure she would hear it. She strode into the dining room and announced that she thought she'd heard a motor in the room and could smell oil fumes. Our colleagues kept a straight face and denied it all.

When she eventually left, we rode out into the lift to depart. A young man lay on a stretcher inside, and he turned out to be the person Maddy had had a date with the night before. He was in a lot of pain with a broken leg and thought he was hallucinating when he had to share the lift with us perched on a scooter!

That scenario pretty much set the scene for fun years to come, until the inevitability of marriage and family forced us to modify our behavior. The irony is that the two most lawless girls in Townsville both married lawyers.

Anyone who meets Maddy can't help but be impressed by her appearance, poise and astuteness. They may also learn that she is a musician, artist, sculptor and superb cook. We have two mutual friends who call themselves Worker Bee and Queen Bee. I think it would be appropriate to call us Glamorous Bird and Dull Bird—at least in our appearances. I'm sure I don't have to tell you who the Dull Bird is.

3. Barcelona

'Go placidly amidst the noise and haste and remember what peace there may be in silence.' Desiderata. Max Ehrmann. 1927

My first encounter with Spain was in Barcelona, the capital of Catalonia, located on the north east of Spain on the coast of the Mediterranean. Barcelona is a city of immeasurable culture: art galleries, architecture, museums, history, music, and fabulous food. A fitting location for the start of my journey.

The city lived up to and exceeded my expectations, assaulting my senses with a constant cacophony of colour, sounds, smells, tastes and sights—especially the exuberant and juicy architecture. Unfettered by a tyrannical beaurocracy, the city let rip on every level and managed to remain, at the same time, gentle and civilized. This was one full-blooded, vibrant city with so much to see and absorb. I found it, in a very sweet way … overwhelming.

I felt so alive with the profusion of beauty so close at hand. My neck became sore and strained by constantly looking up. Bodies bumped into me, but nothing could persuade me to look straight ahead or at the ground.

The locals who became exasperated when we couldn't understand their language just shouted louder and louder, apparently believing that an increase in volume equated to an increase in comprehension.

Walking through the old city, taking in the ambiance, one could conjure up all that had transpired in that small space: Roman domination; Catholic domination; domination of the Americas. It all reeked of domination. Not in the usual detrimental way but with a flamboyance that rendered it forgivable.

My son, Dan, an excellent architect, has always been passionate about the Spanish architect Gaudi, who was best known for his modernistic architecture. Gaudi's work transcended the modernism of his day, combining architecture, religion, and nature to produce creations that reflect those passions. I'd only ever seen Gaudi in books and had formed the opinion that he was decidedly self-indulgent and sloppy in his design. I've always embraced a stringently balanced and minimalist approach to design and life generally—I like to travel lightly, instantly jettisoning anything I perceive as clutter. Spain was about to turn that on its head … starting with Gaudi.

The Sagrada Familia Basilica in Barcelona is the most highly recognized of Gaudi's works, unfinished as it is. When I'd seen it in books, I'd always been tempted to take out the clippers and trim it up. It looked like a fruit tree that hadn't been pruned—ever! With all sorts of aberrations dangling from every nook and cranny.

Only when I entered that sacred space did I start to understand the profundity of what he'd built—a big, cool, extravagant space that boastfully displayed the mysteries of the universe. The droves of visitors, who talk in hushed tones, are supplied with earphones that deliver a commentary that ingeniously takes them through the deeper levels and meanings of the design. I found myself riveted on the spot—with about fifty spots to go—going deeper and deeper into this amazing space. I won't go into the Gaudi mission now, I was astonished by his intellect and spirituality.

The markets, another unforgettable experience, boasted rack upon rack of fresh vegetables, seafood, cheeses and bread. I wondered when the locals found enough time to consume all that the markets offered. Food choices also overwhelmed me—so much fresh produce and preserves. I soon found out that available time is not a problem for the Spanish. One of the cornerstones of their culture is the daily ritual of Siesta. Every day they start work at 9 a.m. and close down at 2 p.m., supposedly to open up again at 4 p.m. In the rural areas, however, the 4 p.m. opening is quietly forgotten. The reason for this practice is that Spain has a very hot climate. Also, the midday hours are used for eating the main meal of the day, washed down with wine and followed by a sleep. A lovely way to live, but I couldn't help but think about the effect on the productivity of the entire country.

In Barcelona, in the Cathedral of the Holy Cross, we picked up our credential books: a passport-sized book that serves as a pilgrim's passport when seeking to stay in the various albergues and hostels along the Way. In existence since the medieval times, they are stamped at whatever albergue you stay in to verify your status as a pilgrim. Though a dull little book to start with, they soon become very beautiful, decorated with ancient spiritual and religious symbols stamped on, just like regular passports, with the dates indicating your last place or stopover. Each town and albergue have different art work representing their place in history. Because we walked two Caminos, we ended up with two credencial books. They remain two of my cherished possessions.

Maddy and I passed a fabulous three days in Barcelona. We travelled well together, liking the same food, music and almost anything else that friends can share. I never imagined that two weeks later we'd split up and go our separate ways, torn apart by the unrelenting, grueling nature of our quest and of Type 1 diabetes.

Barcelona Markets **Old Town**

Los Ramblas

Window detail

Backstreets

La Sagrada Familia Exterior   La Sagrada Familia Interior

4. Montserrat

'Music is the art of the prophets, the only art that calms the agitations of the soul.' Martin Luther, 1483-1546

Leaving Barcelona proved difficult. The original path now ran along a very busy highway, complete with semi-trailers and frenetic traffic. We opted for a cab ride to the start of the trail in a charming beech forest and fell into our usual style of walking, slightly separated and lost in our thoughts. This first day finished rather unceremoniously in a Holiday Inn with pervasive air conditioning, bar fridge and an ancient TV with thirty-eight channels all speaking Spanish. We drowned our disappointment in the accommodation with the contents of the bar fridge. An industrial estate had covered the original pilgrim's accommodation, an albergue, with tar and cement. On the second day, we left the highway and entered some very sweet oak forests. The distances between villages became longer.

On the third day of the Camino Catalonia, Maddy and I found ourselves at the base of a mountain that appeared to be sheer vertical rock, tapering off slightly at the top. This was the legendary Montserrat Monastery. Sixty kilometers west of Barcelona, atop a 1,200 metre mountain, its official Benedictine name is the Monastery de Santa Maria.

Like so many significant religious/spiritual sites in Europe, the Montserrat Mountain was in use earlier than Christianity. The Romans had built a temple to Venus on that site. The first mention of Christianity was in 888. The Benedictines rebuilt it after Napoleon's troops destroyed it in 1811. Currently, it's a fully functioning small village, boasting a world-famous choir, a school for music and the celebrated Black Madonna. The usual access routes are by car or cable car, but for those doing the pilgrimage, the narrow path up the face of the very steep mountain was the only acceptable course. If we didn't climb that, we wouldn't be eligible to stay overnight in the monastery.

For me, that didn't present a problem as I've spent much of my life climbing mountains—a strange indulgence. I feel that this compulsion came about as a result of a childhood spent in outback Queensland, suffocating in the flat, featureless plains only occasionally alleviated by the flat-top mesas. When we were kids, when driving past these mesas, Mum would stop and open the car door, and we'd charge up to the top as fast as our skinny, dusty legs would carry us.

Maddy, on the other hand, was not enthralled with the idea. Her forte was the long flat plains that formed at least 75% of the journey. When I reminded her that we were retracing the steps that pilgrims and those before them had taken for millennia, we strode off under the searing heat of the Spanish sun.

I relished the climb, feeling as if I'd sprouted wings, flying higher and higher, sweat pouring from face and limbs. I didn't want to stop, not even to look at the panorama opening up behind me. This feeling is often spoken of by athletes and mountaineers—a peak experience when the body feels potent and thoroughly synchronized with the mind and spirit.

Eventually, we arrived at the top. The monastery soared above us, very stern and imposing, a building designed to reflect power and discipline, constructed from large stone blocks without evident flaws. A tall, pencil-thin monk, who was one of the most handsome men I'd seen for a very long time, showed us to our accommodation. Maddy and I irreverently declared him a manifestation of wasted manhood. The appropriately Spartan cells held six rusty old bunk beds. I've slept in some austere places in my life, but the WWII ticking mattresses on the sagging wire bunks came as a surprise—it wasn't the last time this sinking feeling would inform our bodies and minds of a hard night ahead. However, weariness has a way of smoothing the lumps and bumps of the roughest of bedding.

When the bells rang for evening vespers, in response to their potent lure and despite the exhausted state of our legs, we literally ran to the Chapel of Santa Cecelia and forced open the two massive and ancient timber doors—not dissimilar to the doors we Catholic children saw on our holy cards representing the gates of heaven. The human oils, blood, sweat and tears of a thousand years of worship had passed into them and rendered them a dark mahogany color. We entered into the cool, dimly lit space, and only in the flicker of innumerable candles, could we see the architectural miracle of layers of Romanesque detail. We jostled to get as close as we could to the altar.

The L'Escolania Choir, an all-male choir comprised of both adults and children—from the boys studying at the boarding school—sang vespers, accompanied by the smell of incense, the occasional cough, and the unconscious shuffling movement of the congregation rearranging their bodies.

I found myself standing in awe, my body responding to the voices by sending shivers up my spine. The power of the human voice used in the correct way is transformative, sending the mind and soul either to dizzying heights or the depths of despair. The quality of this choir's voices sent most of the congregation into raptures, despite the fact that most of them had probably never set a foot inside a church for many years—if at all. They were day trippers who'd spilled from the buses, those who didn't have to climb up the mountain. I became aware of a little elitism creeping into my mind and gave myself a quick slap on the back of my hand.

After an evening of sacred music, we bedded down to our less-than-salubrious accommodation only to have our peace broken by a Viking—a crazy Nordic-type woman from Iceland who shared our room. Sabine, a large, six-foot tall blonde of German origin, was Wagnerian in physical proportions and personal space, and she appeared to have no control over her unbridled passions for smoking and drinking—not the sort of thing one would expect in a medieval monastery.

I instantly took to her as a source of entertainment and spontaneity. Maddy, on the other hand, could see that she was a disaster about to happen. Apart from her constant chain smoking, she also carried the biggest and heaviest pack we'd seen so far. Most walkers reduce the contents of their packs to the minimum, but this girl had the most extraordinary array of paraphernalia in hers. This included shot glasses, a heavy duty, very large padlock, books, journals and more. As a very experienced walker, Maddy was appalled. I, however, enjoyed her eccentricities. Though we'd always been close friends and remain so, we differ in some areas.

So much happened that I had to absorb and process on that very first day: the steep climb; the standard of the accommodation; the effect the choir had on me, and the sheer volume of history, culture and music. I went to bed with my legs enjoying the afterglow of a challenging climb, but my mind raced and I tossed and turned on that prickly horse-hair mattress. Exhaustion took over, however, and sleep came readily. My last thoughts were wondering how many other pilgrims had lain on this mattress, cursed its lumps and bumps and scratched at the itchiness delivered by horse hair.

Sculpture on mountain

Walking into the sunrise

Crucifix   View from cloister

5. Camino Catalan

'To take the road less traveled.' M. Scott Peck

After three glorious days in Barcelona and one day and night in Montserrat, it was time to move on and cover some serious distance. We would've stayed longer in Montserrat, but the rules for staying in albergues stipulate that pilgrims can only stay one night. In that narrow window of opportunity, we explored every nook and cranny. Many places deserved days of probing, but we simply didn't have time. We had 1,300 kilometres between our current location and our destination. I chose not to dwell on this for obvious reasons.

The morning of our departure delivered an amazingly red sunrise accompanied by another choir. This time it was the small seed birds that are plentiful in Spain. They had so much to celebrate and made sure that we heard about it before we departed.

Catalonia, because of its geographical location on the Mediterranean, has been the first stop of the military, ideological and cultural waves over the centuries. One of Spain's richest and highly industrialized regions, it is well pleased with its identity and language and remains independent minded. In the 15th century, Catalonia became part of Spain when King Ferdinand of Aragon married Queen Isabella of Castille, uniting the realms.

There has always been a strong separatist movement which has recently intensified because of the GFC. Luckily for us, no one rioted during our stay.

Many of the numerous small towns and villages, however, had an overwhelming feel of decay and showed no outward signs of modernity. Buildings and walls crumbled over a history going back to the Visigoths. The walls revealed the layers of history in the fabrics used to build them, from the very rough, uneven stonework used in the period B.C. up to the top levels that display stonework as an art form. They reminded me of the rings of a tree trunk demonstrating time lapses, famine and bountiful eras.

Approaching them after hours of walking, we first heard the dogs barking, then saw a few cars and then the townsfolk ignoring us or maybe shrugging their shoulders. When we eventually found a food outlet, desperately hungry, the only thing on offer was the usual bocadillo—a baguette sandwich—washed down with cold beer. Not that we complained; any food was a wondrous outcome in a place where most people were enjoying their siesta.

The architecture of these small villages sometimes reminded me of those derelict Mexican towns that Hollywood movies so regularly depict, but thankfully without the gratuitous shooting and killing. Sleeping yellow dogs, sleeping donkeys, and sleeping people complete the vision. The occupants are somnolent and withdrawn. This is a seriously unvisited part of Spain. I was starting to think that 'out of order' was Spanish for computer. Every computer for weeks on end bore that distinguished title—in English no less. We made sure we didn't linger too long in these places, worrying that the tiredness would dwindle into our souls and drain what little energy we had at the end of a long hard day.

I shaded my eyes with my hand and scanned the flat, dusty land around us. The landscape through which we walked consisted of endless pastoral or agricultural farmland lined by irrigation canals. I rested under the only tree in that vast monotonous plain and could only see Maddy ahead of me by the dust she kicked up. I wondered what had been here before industrialized agriculture impacted on it—maybe a forest of elder, oak, or ash trees. Could such trees have been cut down to build the Armada? If so what a tragedy of farcical proportions.

Unfortunately for me, though I could see the snow-capped Pyrenees in the distance, the mind-numbing monotony of walking across this boring flat land combined with soaring temperatures—thirty-eight degrees on many days—made this a particularly challenging two weeks.

The large number of paved roads and highways along which we walked created an additional problem. The hard surfaces combined with the heat caused our feet to swell and blood blisters to emerge. The terrain reminded me of outback Australia, flat and dry with mirages shimmering on the horizon.

I dealt with this dry heat by jumping fully dressed into the irrigation canals to cool off. My soaking clothes quickly turned back to crisp, crackling fabric. Another way I counteracted this discomfort was to mentally dwell on the cool, snow-covered mountains where I've spent so much of my life. In an effort to neutralise my aversion to hot, dry and flat land, I fantasized that I could grow wings and soar across to Chamonix—not far if one could fly there!

A chance encounter with an American couple, however, relieved the monotony of this lonely stretch. They were researching the effects pilgrims had on the local community, but so few pilgrims walked this part of the journey that I don't think they even put pen to paper on that stretch of road. The first English-speaking people we'd encountered since leaving Barcelona, Dan and Ellen provided an oasis of good conversation and companionship. Though we only walked together for a few days, we shared many life stories and experiences, and our discussions ran all day and halfway through the night. They were mountaineers from Oregon and shared my dislike of flat ground. This was my first taste of the eclectic mix of people you could meet on a daily basis. They ranged from friendly, ascetic, obnoxious, irritating, rude, interesting, intellectual, arrogant, zealous, slack, immoral, saintly, fat, thin, tall, short, beautiful, ugly and aloof, but never boring!

Dan and Ellen were the first and two of the more memorable pilgrims we were to meet.

Hot white road

Dan and Ellen

Streetscape

Street Sign

6. The Road to Pamplona

'A lone walker is both present and detached, more than an audience, but less than a participant. Walking assuages or legitimizes this alienation.' Rebecca Solnit

Few pilgrims walked this part of the Camino, so we spent most days walking alone, which brings on its own reward. Our Viking friend had dropped back, and I missed her ribald humour, but Maddy was well and truly over her by this stage, so we tried to outwalk her. Her determination was flawless, though. She forced her eighty kilos, unfit frame to fly over the hills, reminding me of the significance of one's DNA.

I got to know Sabine very well. Born in post-war Germany, the progeny of a German mother and Russian father, she had suffered as a child and carried the inevitable scars. What I loved about her was her excruciating honesty and a willingness to move on from her wounded childhood. We shared many a good night on the town, including Saturday night rages until dawn.

Maddy was a much faster walker and waited for me to share coffee and meal breaks. As we settled into the rhythm and flow of daily walking, I found this journey to be somewhat of an emotional roller coaster. As a child I'd learned to walk in the deserts of outback Australia. I loved my environment and walked for hours, losing myself on treeless plains that seemed to stretch to infinity. This all changed when I experienced the verdant landscape of the coast, and I developed an addiction to moist, green rolling hills and cool, crisp alpine areas. On the Camino I found myself doing long periods of tiresome trudging along hot dusty roads in a stultifying landscape of sameness, repeating 'What am I doing here?' over and over in my head. I, as someone who finds joy in the cold pristine surroundings of an alpine region, found it psychologically torturous. But there was a flip side to this: the mental and physical pain pushed one inside, creating an interior spiritual journey with vivid moments of transformation. I found this the most difficult part of the journey.

After a long hot walk, around the next bend, we would walk into a quaint medieval village with architectural oddities, good coffee and a seat under a shade tree where we would always elevate our legs, much to the consternation of the locals. The locals weren't always welcoming and saw us quite often as a nuisance, particularly when we asked for something as extraordinary as a bocadillo after midday. The ever-present yellow dogs, however, always greeted us, tails wagging in expectation of a morsel kindly dropped at our feet. I often wonder why poor areas of the world nearly always have an abundance of yellow dogs. Whether in Laos, Indonesia, Venezuela, India or Africa, there are always these incredibly tough and skinny animals. My heart always goes out to them.

Every town was unique. Many perched atop the hills, surrounded by colossal thick stone walls and battlements. I learned that they sought high ground to gain military advantage in the perpetual regional warmongering and the even-more-serious threat of the Ottoman Empire.

Exploring the world on foot is a good way of realizing the enormity of our planet, and the infinite possibilities of our minds. The simplicity of our days, reduced to the basic needs of shelter, food and water—such a drastic change from the hustle and bustle of regular life at home—had a liberating effect on one's mind. No deadlines, no commitments, no external demands; all day to walk, think, sing and sometimes talk.

The evening meals were always a delight: local produce washed down with copious amounts of *vino tinto*. Despite the lure of the lively company and conversations on offer, I often felt too exhausted to expend any energy in small talk in broken English.

Though not popular and not frequently taken, The Camino Catalan did have its highlights. Though still in the Provence of Aragon, lush fields, crystal-clear rivers, dark forests and snow-covered mountains in the distance replaced the harsh dry landscape.

As we walked through the sublime vistas of this luscious place with its rare balance of wet and dry, I couldn't help but dwell on the fate of Catherine of Aragon, the loyal and devout first wife of King Henry VIII. For a political agenda, she was plucked from this wonderful environment only to be married off to the then King of England—a psychopath in some people's estimate. Not only her husband but also the dreary and constantly wet landscape of England must have taken a toll on her heart and soul. A lesser character couldn't have maintained her dignity and sense of decency. She was, after all, the daughter of Isobel and Ferdinand, both warriors of impeccable calibre.

After overnighting in Santa Cruz de la Seros, we climbed up the track through the forest to arrive at San Juan de la Pena.

This religious complex consisted of two structures. The old monastery, built in 920 in Romanesque style is partially carved into the stone of the great cliff that overhangs the foundation. Legend has it that the Chalice of the Last Supper (Holy Grail) was sent there to be protected from the Muslim invaders of the Iberian Peninsula. After the fire of 1675, a new monastery was built on a higher level. This Benedictine establishment was the last in Spain to use the Latin Mass. That doesn't surprise me as it's in such a remote and isolated part of Spain. This place had an almost mystical presence and although there are few people around these days, it must have been the stage of much drama and upheaval, both religious and military.

Old Monastery

Early Christian symbols

Early Christian symbols

Wife farewelling her crusader husband

 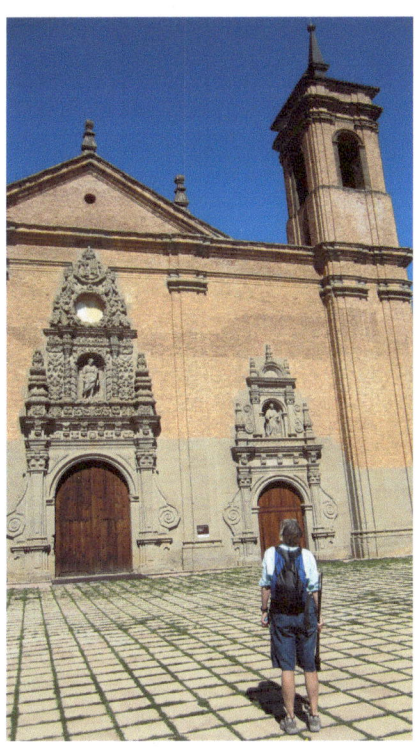

Angel of Death　　　　The Author at New Monastery

Ploughed Fields

7. The Lurking Menace Strikes Again

'Great perils have their beauty, that they bring to light the fraternity of strangers.' Victor Hugo.

Insulin-dependent diabetics shouldn't do certain things! I found out the hard way that walking for six to eight hours per day carrying a fourteen-kilogram pack was one of them. The relentless routine sent me into a state of ketoacidosis, which makes it almost impossible to eat because the stomach shuts down and nausea prevails. Diabetic ketoacidosis is life-threatening. It occurs when the body cannot process glucose, so it begins to break down fat and muscle for energy. The by-product is ketones (fatty acid) and upon entering the bloodstream these cause a chemical imbalance.

I found myself replenishing my body with beer. Light, easy to digest and lots of feel-good factor. By ten days into our journey, I had reduced my insulin requirements by 90% and still consumed massive amounts of glucose in the form of jelly snakes to stave off hypoglycemic (low blood-sugar level) episodes. I hadn't realized until then just how much those snakes weigh. When you're throwing away underwear to reduce the weight, four bags of snakes weigh a ton.

One day we set out to do a ten-hour walk. I loaded myself up with five bags of snakes and two cans of coke, which under normal circumstances would've sent me into a hyperglycemic (high blood-sugar levels) coma.

When we came across the mountains, enthralled by the stunning scenery wrapped in mist, I embraced the climb with the fervour of a lover. Before I reached the top, however, the hypo hit, with its familiar intense hunger, a sense of anxiety, diminishing vision and an overwhelming feeling of dread. I consumed every bit of carbohydrate I had with me, but still the levels spiralled downwards, out of control. I'd been on my own for at least an hour in a very remote part of Spain. My body had shed large amounts of water through perspiration, so I was ringing wet, and my vision faded to the stage where I looked at the world through a small round space (tunnel vision). As far as I knew, no one was less than a half hour behind me. I didn't panic, however; I just sat on the side of the road, not concerned about passing away but worried about the mess it would leave for my family—collecting the body from the other side of the world and so on. I felt enormous remorse.

Then, as happened so often on this journey, the angels stepped in! Two young girls appeared out of the mist. By that stage, I was sitting on a rock fighting to maintain consciousness, and they came to my rescue with four juice poppers. My hands shook when I grabbed the sweet drinks from them. Ever so slowly life ebbed back into my body, although I was most likely in a state of shock. Little did the young German girls know the significance of what they'd done—saved a silly old woman from oblivion!

That was not the only episode of severe hypoglycemia I experienced. Many things seriously tested me, but it wasn't the heat, the distance, the bed bugs, the blood blisters, feral albergue managers, the hacked email or the cancelled Visa but the metabolic meltdown that was the most insurmountable and deadly of all the challenges I had thrown at me on this journey. Luckily, only a few of us have to endure and outwit it.

At this stage, out of respect for my dear companion, and with a heavy heart, I decided to part company with Maddy. I could see that my need to stop and rest with my flagging health and bleeding, blistered and painful feet frustrated her. She had a strict schedule to stick to, and I was a millstone around her neck. I started to feel like someone portrayed in those medieval religious murals full of long faces and suffering that are plentiful in this part of Spain! At least tears were allowed on the religious statues.

I'd grown up in a part of Australia that had a particularly harsh environment. The predominately Scottish settlers had managed to survive and flourish in a desert that even the local Aborigines shunned. The stoic ways of the Scottish settlers did not allow for tears. They were seen as an outward expression of weakness, a loss of face and source of shame. If one had tears needing to be shed, one did it privately, shared only with your horse, dog or pet lamb. I found myself with the slightest tinge of envy when I saw that the Spanish madonnas and saints could let loose with their tears, some even sporting blood red ones—so much pain, grief, and guilt, all in the pursuit of sanctity. I was very short on sanctity but didn't see the point of trying to stay moving at Maddy's pace—a pace that would guarantee a place in heaven!

She was very fit and had trained hard while I was hobbling around in a moon boot. I'll never forget that sinking feeling of concern for her and my isolation on the rainy morning when she started out on her own to cross the next mountain range. It was cold and misty and after we said our goodbyes, I watched her cross the road, and that familiar blue pack slowly disappeared.

There I was in a remote area of a strange country with no language skills, no maps and nothing to guide me but the rare roadside marker of the cockleshell and the yellow arrow. At times like this, I remind myself of my great grandfather who left behind a lush and verdant landscape of the UK to venture into the outback of Australia. He went by horse and cart from Melbourne to the North West of Queensland, building dams and sinking bores for the early pioneers. Those early pioneers were industrious, self-reliant, visionary and gritty. His efforts have always humbled me, and I chide myself if I don't cope well with the small frustrations faced by modern-day travellers.

I did, however, start to feel that I was involved in a doomed enterprise.

8. Jaca

'Give a girl the right shoes and she can conquer the world.'
Marilyn Monroe

At the risk of being disrespectful, I have to admit that the closest I got to my personal God on this journey was in an air-conditioned bus. After a childhood spent in Catholic boarding schools, I became spiritually aroused and curious about other religions. I delved into Hinduism, Marxism, Scientology, Yoga, Zoroastrianism and any other belief system that presented itself to me, as did many of my generation in the 70's when we abandoned our old belief systems in favour of the more exotic ones. I was awash with options. None of the above held my interest for long, but that changed when I came across Buddhism.

The approach of the Buddhist belief system seemed so natural, unrepressed and instinctive, unconstrained by the dogmas of other religions. It called for rigorous mental inquiry, scrutiny and discipline. I immersed myself totally in Buddhism for thirty years—and still counting. That's not to say that I don't still have a strong appreciation of the Catholic faith and what it has contributed to Western civilisation. The music that resonates with me most are pre-reformation sacred pieces, and I have a continuing fascination with the sacred text. Writers like Thomas Merton and Thomas Aquinas sit comfortably on my book shelves alongside Yogic teachers like BKS Iyengar and the Buddhist mentors Jack Cornfield and Larry Rosenberg. My personal God would most probably not line up with the mainstream vision. My personal God is not harsh, rigid, jealous, judgemental and using guilt to manipulate us all—not at all. My God is humorous, pragmatic, sensitive, compassionate, forgiving and will continue to remain a mystery.

After two weeks of foot slogging across barren, hot plains, my feet told me, 'Enough is enough.' The blisters on my toes had turned into deep-purple, open wounds and my feet screamed for relief. I'd promised myself that the first indication of infection would have me on the next plane home. Travel lore is littered with stories of insulin-dependent diabetics who lose their lower limbs to some exotic bug that has entered an open wound. It was time for me to reassess how I was travelling—hammering myself from dawn to dusk, day after day.

The 'real pilgrims' frown down on anyone who takes this journey by any other means than walking. It's even considered 'not Kosher' to ride a horse, donkey or bike, although a lot of people do. What surprised me is that even in this day and age, there are those who have this medieval mindset that thinks that a pilgrimage has to be accompanied by suffering. The ethos was *so* Catholic, so strongly ascetic—mortification of the flesh, whether you wanted it or not!

I didn't have access to horses, donkeys or bikes, so chose the local bus. But that was pure heresy! Other pilgrims repeatedly told me that one must 'suffer' on the Camino to gain brownie points in the spiritual realm. I seriously didn't get it. There is enough suffering back at home; one does not need to travel halfway across the world to find it; the bastard will find you wherever you may seek to hide.

So after enjoying the ambiance of yet another rustic, medieval village, I climbed aboard the bus, feeling the thrill of a naughty child wagging school. I had no qualms about being a fake pilgrim. As I climbed on board the battered old bus, the first thing I noticed was the air conditioning, and I felt immediate relief from the thirty-eight-degree days we'd had on the treeless plains. My body went limp with unexpected comfort. I felt the cool air wrapping itself around my face then descending down to my sunburnt limbs. What an amazing experience was this cool, comfortable capsule of metal that plummeted across the barren plains. I felt euphoric. Weeks later, when asked if I felt guilty, thankfully, I could reply, 'No.' Guilt is one aspect of Catholicism I discarded years ago, recognizing it as a total waste of emotional energy.

While enjoying the luxury of a dilapidated old bus, I thanked God for the mundane and utilitarian internal-combustion engine. The savior of bleeding and broken feet. So the experience did have some spiritual integrity.

The bus station sat imposingly in the center of a town with a very tall clock tower. The hands of the large tower clock always ran an hour late—a common and very Spanish experience. Somehow the locals worked their way around it. No one could ever accuse them of sweating the small stuff.

The bus dropped me off in Jaca, the first capital of the small mountain kingdom of Aragon, founded in the 11th century. This medieval city also served as a mountain resort, being located so close to the Pyrenees.

In Jaca I managed to buy a pair of Teva adventure sandals. Tevas are a robust synthetic sandal designed for long distance walking. I walked the next 800 kilometres in these, and my feet gradually healed—thanks to the everyday miracles of technology.

I'd spent most of my life in sturdy hiking boots or running shoes with orthotics, so the thought of walking more than two kilometers in these flimsy sandals was pure heresy. But, as it turned out, they saved my feet and my journey. After all this time, I can't bring myself to throw them out! Sitting in my comfortable home now, I often glance across at the worn-out old sandals and think of what we shared.

I became at ease with my heresy, a most-beneficial concept that allows much leeway, a margin of freedom in one's pursuits. Goethe once said, 'I hate everything that merely instructs me, without augmenting or directly invigorating my activities.'

The Catholic Church was hell-bent on eliminating heresy during the Inquisition, I'm afraid they failed. It's alive and well and gets a lot of use on the Camino.

9. Sanguesa

'Hell hath no fury like a woman scorned.' William Congreve.

Having just survived many serious hypoglycemic episodes in one day, after ten hours of walking, I found myself in Sanguesa, a medium-sized town with stunning wooden architecture.

Like most pilgrims, I went straight to the albergue to wash away the trials of the day and waited with the usual line up of weary travelers, all too tired to do much but prop themselves up against the wall. One unusual couple stood out: a very tall, blonde German woman and a minute Japanese lady, both well into their advancing years. I discovered later over a shared meal that they'd met each other on the Way. The German lady told of how she'd survived the incendiary bombings of Germany in 1944, and the tiny Japanese woman who sat demurely and said little had been a survivor of Hiroshima. I couldn't confirm these stories, but they show how the horrors of war melt away on this journey. Despite that Germany and Japan were on the same side inWW2, these women lived worlds apart. However, they experienced the same burden of the post war catastrophes and shame. The fact that these two women had survived so much horror when they were children and in the later stages of their life came together in Spain gives us all hope for the future.

Alburgues are an entity in themselves and without them, many would not be able to make the pilgrimage. They are the lifeblood and backbone of the Way, providing affordable accommodation for thousands of travelers.

The grade of the albergues are not evident until one has checked in. They range from the grandeur of Montserrat Monastery to quaint and rustic villas, and descend to something that almost resembles a concentration camp or an establishment left over from the Stalin era.

This day we had the latter. I felt it the minute I saw pilgrims lined up outside, waiting in silence. Gone was the hum of a conversation brimming with candour. The sun beat down and the dust swirled. A stray cat occupied the only shady place. It sat there like a sphynx, aloofly regarding us with disdain. Sweat ran down my legs, and the only thing on my mind was a vision of a cold shower. I felt the sort of weariness that sinks into the bone marrow.

The deranged albergue manager—a man of about thirty years of age—let us in and started the check-in. Rude from the start, he wore a permanent scowl accompanied by a prominent vein on his forehead that threatened to explode any minute. 'Line up, line up; passports; passports,' he screamed at us.

I couldn't believe what I witnessed. His aggression was beyond anything tolerable. His first act of brutality was to scream at the two older women to take their boots outside. This caused embarrassment to those otherwise stately women and all present. Then one by one he screamed for our passports and credential books. What should have taken fifteen minutes became hours of abuse. I was the last in line, getting angrier and angrier and angrier. By the time I reached him, I felt incandescent with rage—not very pilgrim like! When he started to scream, before the first of his spittle landed on the table, I let out the most blood-curdling scream, then I told him to 'sit down, shut up and sign the BLOODY book.'

The bully immediately turned white with shock, sat down and literally huddled over the register in complete silence! His prior high-colour demeanour turned into a pale shade of watery milk. I felt as though my throat was bleeding, but if it was, not a drop of blood was wasted. I've mentioned the power of the human voice, but unlike the angelic power of choirs and sacred singers, this sounded like a screech from the depths of hell!

The bully then left the building and didn't return until after we'd all left the next day. I found out later that he's a legend in his mistreatment of guests and normally hangs around till nine in the evening harassing everyone.

This was one place I wasn't sad to leave, but maybe in future that little creep will prick his ears when he hears Australia mentioned.

'Oh! Do you come from a land down under, where women glow and men plunder? Can't you hear, can't you hear the thunder; you better run, you better take cover.'

Evil depicted on church door

Santa Maria la Real

Empty marketplace

10. Pamplona

'Be not inhospitable to strangers, lest they be Angels in disguise.'
W.B. Yeats.

Three weeks into the journey I found myself on the French Way, entering the legendary city of Pamplona, an ancient city in the Basque region. The city is well known for the 'Running of the Bulls,' a spectacle that, thankfully, I was too early to witness. Personally, I feel that this is an event that allows the much-put-upon bulls of Spain to get some revenge on those who've spent centuries gaining delight from watching their slow and agonizing death in the arena. During the blood-soaked fiesta in San Fermin, bulls die sometimes as many as eight per day in the bull ring. The Pamplona ring appropriately boasts the statue of Ernest Hemingway, the secular patron saint of machismo. When I walked past this edifice, I felt the bile rise in my throat, in disgust at that enduring spectacle of animal cruelty.

However, the suffering of bulls was the last thing on my mind as I staggered into the town centre very late in the day, looking for accommodation. Rain poured down, and my small map started to deteriorate. I went from albergue to albergue only to be told that there was no room. The usual commercial accommodation venues were also full.

Spanish street names are written in *very* small print on a tiled plaque and placed high on the walls of a building. Unlike our street names, such as Queen Street or Martin Place, these read more like a biography of some prominent historical person, such as Don Miguel de Navarra—who killed two thousand Moors, had six children, enjoyed jousting and had one leg longer than the other.

Exuberant revelry marked the day as part of a normal weekend in Spain. No one spoke English, of course, nor French, nor German, and the jostling crowd of partygoers was mostly very drunk and raucous. I felt like an invisible, very fragile leaf being tossed around in a gale of pressing humanity.

I hadn't felt so totally alone and confused, a strange person in a strange land, for a long time, but the familiar feelings of anxiety rose in my stomach as I lurched around in the hard rain.

Lost in misery, I stood on the corner of the road, and out of nowhere, a tiny nun appeared in her black habit and veil, which somehow protected her from the human maelstrom. Without saying a word, she took me by the hand and walked me across the city to a very large albergue, where I at last found a bed. I felt so intensely secure and confident in her hands, and yet because of her stooped posture and veil, I didn't even see her face. Not a word passed between us, and to this day I often wonder if perhaps she was some sort of angel. Tradition tells us that angels are sent to pilgrims struggling on the Camino. I didn't embrace Shirley MacLaine's approach to this venture, where you wrestle with angels and demons on a daily basis and sup with Merlin at night. But I have to admit that sometimes serendipitous things happened—usually at a point of utter hopelessness, when all the everyday defenses were down.

Having found a roof over my head, I ventured into the narrow streets of the city, taking in the ambiance. The crowd was friendly and in the mood for a typical Spanish Saturday night. In the 19th century cafés, older locals huddled in small groups, sipping their café con leche, totally oblivious to the swarming tourists. I supped with strangers on the ever-present tuna salad and *vino tinto*, then I sallied forth until well after midnight, observing the constant carnival antics. I was still traveling on my own, and no one would have noticed a little old lady lurking in the shadows. It was the best night of voyeurism I had. It was also the last, as I was about to join a group of fun-loving people on the next stage of my journey. That was when I became one of the festive crowd.

The following morning, I decided to catch an early bus out of the city to the next small village. Sunday mornings in Spain are utterly devoid of activity as the Saturday night festivities usually last until sunrise.

Once again, I found myself adrift and disorientated, looking for the bus station to take me past the ugly industrial outskirts of the city to the nearest small village. Industrial areas are as displeasing to the eye in Spain as they are elsewhere in the world. The only thing to keep me company was the clicking of my metal poles on the cobblestoned road. Not a soul in sight. Then, it happened again!

An elderly gentleman who spoke perfect English offered to take me to the bus station. It turned out that he was a professor of History at the local university, and as we walked, he pointed out all the places of historical significance, describing how the Roman General Pompeii had built this city in 74 B.C. and pointing out where the original walls still stood. I expected Mary Beard to jump out at me anytime. He delivered me safely to the bus and waited until I boarded. Definitely not an angel, but a superb human being.

That period of fewer than eighteen hours in Pamplona was full of intense positive and negative emotion, confusion and pleasant surprises—fairly typical of a day on the Camino.

Dwelling in Old Pamplona

Pharmacy in Pamplona Old Town

No bulls today

11. Scientists, Spanish Grandmothers, & Other Useful Angels

'A kind gesture can reach a wound that only compassion can heal.'
Steve Maraboli.

As I have mentioned before, despite the unexpected challenges thrown at pilgrims, someone was always at hand to help. Guardian Angels, some would say. They came from all parts of the globe—South Africa, USA, France, Brazil, Mexico, Argentina, Iceland, England, Scotland, Ireland, Germany, not to mention the Spanish.

I found myself on the receiving end of help so often that I felt chuffed when the chance to render assistance to others came. All my life, I have been a carer, daughter, sister, wife, mother, and nana. My work has been varied, working on the family station as a child, caring for horses, dogs, sheep, cattle and orphaned wild life, followed by nursing, caring for the ill and disabled. Mountain guiding entailed steering people through dangerous storms, blizzards, gale-force winds and difficult-to-navigate landscapes. As a national park ranger, I cared for the environment and animals that dwelt in it. I'm fiercely independent and have always been the care provider, so for me to ask for help was 'to stoop and pick up nothing.' This journey taught me to let go of my pride; I had to. The internal shifts of consciousness and the unexpected relief that followed felt very liberating.

I rapidly became used to the idea of accepting help from others. The intimacy of our situation forced one to get very close to people from all over the world in a way I hadn't experienced on other journeys. On one occasion Mona, a sweet lady from Cape Town, saved my bacon. I met Mona in a café in one of the countless, barren little villages, north of Leon when I was despairing of all the wretched albergues we found ourselves in at night. The only guide I had was a very small book put out by the Michelin marketing team. It displayed the route but didn't advise on the quality of the hostels. Mona had done this journey before, so we sat down over a coffee, went through the book and she outlined the preferred places and crossed out the no-go places. Her prior experience proved invaluable. I found out later, through talking to her friends, that she was a medical-research scientist and had designed a synthetic coronary graft that bodies won't reject—an amazing woman, and so quiet, gentle and caring. She and I spent many an evening on the veranda of cool adobe houses, watching the tall storm clouds roll over the red, parched earth. When big fat drops of rain raised the dust in front of us, producing an exquisite fragrance, we lifted our glasses filled with chilled vino blanc and drank to Spain, with all its beauty, foibles, frustrations, wonders and never-ending surprises.

An experience that endeared me to the Spanish community, happened in a medium-sized city called Astorga. At the end of a long hard day, I was standing in a queue at the EFTPOS machine when a girl made her transaction and pulled out her credit card, but walked off leaving the cash sitting on the machine. Behind her stood a tiny old Spanish lady, complete with her all-pervasive black clothing. She ran down the road in pursuit of the pilgrim, waving the cash in her hands and yelling at full volume. The girl took her cash, overwhelmed with relief and gratitude. The woman's honesty was even more remarkable because it happened in 2012, the year of the Global Financial Crisis (GFC) when riots happened all over Spain and the locals were struggling financially.

I began to realize that almost everyone I met, pilgrims and locals alike, were generous on every level. However, life would be boring without coming across those forlorn souls who display their anger and nastiness arrogantly and without restraint. Like the harbingers of nastiness, they appear when you least expect it. A group of loudly self-declared 'card-carrying communists' harangued anyone within ear distance with their political absolutism. An equally loud group of large South African women with zero tolerance quickly dispensed with them. It seemed that these preachers couldn't let go of their dreary, battered banner, holding it aloft in an ineffectual retreat from the grim awfulness of their lives—the muse and the monsters.

By the time I started on the first week of 'the French Way,' I'd well and truly become learned in protecting and sustaining feet. Education provided by the 'school of the road'—no pun intended.

Every day I found many people in a distressed state about the condition of their feet. Some had already decided to pull out and go home. The younger girls often cried with disappointment. For some obscure reason, walkers are advised to wear heavy hiking boots. Probably because of the initial steep climb and descent on the Pyrenes on the first days of the French route. However, from that point on, the path turns into flat, hard clay or hot asphalt surfaces. Feet get hot, swell up and within hours, enormous blisters build. Years of endurance sports taught me all I needed to know about blisters, both avoiding them and treating them. I also had skills in taping overuse injuries on knees, feet and ankles. I quickly became the 'go to' person for foot and leg injuries. First, I advised them to send their heavy boots back home and purchase a pair of trekking sandals or a pair of regular running shoes.

I felt pleasantly surprised when I ran into those people further down the track and found out that they'd almost completed their venture. Their gratitude was overwhelming, and I felt a little more useful.

12. Logrono

'Walking with a friend in the dark is better than walking alone in the light.' Helen Keller

Once on the French Way, the weather turned from hot and dry to cold and wet—a very welcome change for my dry and blistered skin. The other notable change was the increase in the number of pilgrims with whom I shared the road. The Camino Française is the most popular of all the various routes. Some complain about the crowds, but after spending so much time alone, I found comfort in once again being surrounded by people and listening to the chatter of global travellers.

I continued walking by myself until I met Renate.

I'd booked into a municipal albergue in Logrono as it was the only one left with available beds. I should have known to avoid the wretched places run by local municipalities but was too tired to walk any further. The accommodation consisted of a large bunker housing over 100 pilgrims in double bunks placed up against each other with only enough space to squeeze sideways into your old horsehair mattress. Very small windows at the top of the wall provided inadequate ventilation. The Black Hole of Calcutta—a dungeon in Fort William which held British prisoners of war—came to mind and remained prominent in my thoughts. I almost gagged on the thick atmosphere of unwashed bodies and smelly boots.

While lying there on my lumpy mattress trying to overcome exhaustion, I noticed a woman in the next bunk in distress over the state of her feet. She had very deep blisters that had become infected, and her big, light-blue eyes welled up with tears. After introducing myself, we commiserated together about the blisters and overcrowded conditions. Misery loves company.

That was the start of a wonderful friendship. Renate came from South Africa, and her husband had been brutally murdered in a home invasion—a common occurrence in Cape Town. Renate and I 'just clicked,' and we shared some incredible experiences together over the next four weeks.

She walked the Camino in memory of her late husband, who'd always planned to do it himself. Even though we spent many days walking together, like most pilgrims, we also chose to spend many days walking alone to afford the contemplation so essential on this journey.

I met a lot of South Africans, but not all were as endearing as Renate with her sweet face. I noticed a hard edge about them, but a brief glimpse at their historical circumstances and present-day challenges could explain the reason for that. The Oscar Pistorius trial ran while we walked the Camino, so it was foremost in a lot of discussions. Oscar Pistorius, a leading South African runner who competed in multiple Paralympic games, shot and killed his girlfriend Reeva Steenkamp in his Pretoria home, saying he mistook her for an intruder. The South Africans were almost unanimous about his innocence—citing the very real threat of home invasions in their country—while the rest of the world appeared to have already decided that he was guilty. Food for thought.

The conditions in the albergue were as bad as it gets. The kitchen was filthy, with one young girl tending to her pus-oozing toes on the dining room table where people prepared their evening meals. While third in line to use the showers—only two cubicles for up to 80 guests—I watched with incredulity as the first two girls stood underneath the shower for close to half an hour, taking all the hot water. Indifference to fellow travelers was unusual on the Camino, but these girls took the prize for lack of concern for others—it's a wonder the angry mob didn't lynch them. Only sheer weariness rescued the girls from a potential avalanche of hostility.

With people packed into the dormitory like sardines in a can, the collective snoring sounded so loud that the experience felt akin to an airplane preparing to lift off. One very overweight man in the centre of the dorm snored so loudly that some people threw shoes at him during the night. He woke up covered by shoes and boots that had failed to stir him out of his stupor.

Renate and I stayed awake for a long time, swapping stories about our travel experiences and life in general. I found her a most delightful, intelligent and sensitive person, and I could see that she still wrestled with the untimely and violent death of her husband.

We were both struggling with the hardships of our journey, and at one time considered giving up, but thankfully we learned to support each other and decided to carry on. With my medical background, I could advise her on her badly blistered feet, and her solid good sense and encouragement went a long way to help me stay the course.

The results of the GFC were evident everywhere. However, one day while shuffling along in a dream, we came upon someone's nightmare, a new, empty, purpose-built golf resort. This five-star establishment had five-star accommodation and five-star facilities but no five-star guests. It was a ghost town. We didn't see a soul anywhere! Strangely the lawns were all perfectly mown. Maybe a grumpy old man from Australia had found his paradise of endless acres of lawns to mow with no nagging wife to spoil his abstracted state of absorption.

Now that I was on the most popular part of the Camino—the 'main drag' as we say in Australia—I found companionship on every turn. I was starting to relish the journey. At last the celebrated alchemy of the Camino was working its charm on me, and I looked forward to each and every day that lay ahead.

Meseta

Life long friends

13. As Pants the Hart for Cooling Streams

Psalm 42
'Music is the fourth great material want. First food, then clothes, then shelter, then music.' Christian Nestell Bovee.

The title of this chapter is an exercise in nostalgia. The nuns at my boarding school taught us music, and I enjoyed the choir the most. At a very young age, I learned to love singing sacred music in parts. Psalm 42 was my favourite.

After enduring a lot of unsavory albergues, I found it comforting to arrive at a place of welcome, and I found such a place in the Meseta, a particularly desolate section of the walk. A large, elevated plateau, devoid of vegetation, the Meseta is very hot and very flat, with nowhere to shelter from the relentless sun. The walk across it could drive vulnerable people into the void of insanity, but without it the trip would be incomplete.

Day after day I walked through this landscape, dreaming about Chamonix that lay on the other side of the Alps, and fearful of exposing any part of my body in case the vacuum of this arid place absorbed it never to be seen again. I managed the crossing by getting up at 4.30 am in the relative cool of the morning and, along with the others who took this course of action, usually got to the albergues ahead of our more slothful comrades—though I imagine there isn't any place that Sister Sloth can truly gain purchase on this journey.

One day a group of us arrived at midday at a dismal village that oozed antiquity, desolation and morbidity. It made a B-grade Western Mexican village look like Manhattan! When we arrived at our 'place of shelter,' we faced a two-story, mud-brick building that would look at home in a Hollywood biblical setting of Nazareth or Bethlehem. The handwritten sign declared that it would be open to receive guests at 2 pm.

It was worth the wait!

When they opened, we walked into a pre-fourteenth-century building, wonderfully preserved and with thick walls that guaranteed constant cool. Ancient timber struts composed the walls and heavy beams held up the ceilings. The floor consisted of an ornate pattern of very worn and shiny cobblestones.

Volunteers from Europe with Spanish heritage managed it, mostly university students on their holidays. They told us that our evening meal would be free as long as we all formed a team to cook it. I lucked out, as one of our team was a distinguished chef from New York—my, did we eat that night! I assigned myself to the food prep— chopping and cutting! I like to do the back stage stuff, invisible, enjoying anonymity but managing to be productive at the same time. Our own personal master chef produced a stupendous meal from all locally grown vegetables harvested that day from the surrounding area.

After the meal, various representatives of at least twenty countries were asked to sing a song that their country held dear. This was one of the few occasions in my life that my bravado failed me; I hid when the time came. Have you ever tried to sing the Australian national anthem *Advance Australia Fair* alone before strangers? After the national anthems, we sat around singing and drinking into the wee hours of the day.

I was reminded of what Alison Croggon wrote in her book *The Naming*: 'And all meet in singing, which braids together the different knowings into a wide and subtle music, the music of living.' Croggon's story describes the random nature of this kind of journey; *nothing* is predictable, and that takes away any possibility of banality.

The following day found us in the same routine: up before dawn to beat the heat; starting the walk with an orchestra of birdsong; no one speaking, just enjoying their privacy and the trance one gets into with the most primitive of actions, walking. The days start fresh and cool, but by mid-afternoon one is reduced by loneliness, pain, heat, boredom, and monotony. I entered a zone of sweet vulnerability, where there is nothing more to plan, defend, desire or ache for. The attachments to place, possessions, comfort, luxury, opinions and expectations fell off, one by one.

The singing hostel

Irish Mary, her Camino friend, and the Author

Reception area

14. Leon

'The most eloquent prayer is the prayer through hands that heal and bless.' Billy Graham.

The city of Leon loomed large in our minds as one of the places that demanded a stopover of more than one night. Leon seduced even the most hurried pilgrims, those who vowed never to 'stay a while' to take in the splendor of a place. It also marked the end of the long, hot, dry Meseta, and that came as a relief to us all.

The afternoon I arrived, while standing in the long line of pilgrims waiting to find a bed for the night, I noticed familiar faces. We'd inadvertently formed into groups of disparate people whose only commonality was that we walked the same distance, going in the same direction every day and usually landing at the same albergue. One might think that this would be a flimsy bond, but it turned out to be the cement that bound us.

Irish Mary, a woman from Ireland, had skin so white and devoid of pigment that it never changed colour. While the rest of us turned a dark shade of mahogany due to the relentless, blistering sun, her skin remained almost blue. She was a veteran of the Camino, having spent years bringing groups of teenagers over from Ireland to do part of the journey. Now that she'd retired, she was free to travel independently or with others to enjoy her own journey. She always set out unaccompanied, then would find a 'Camino friend,' usually a mature-aged man who would share the journey with her, no strings attached. I spent a lot of time with Mary; as a practicing Catholic she could refresh the delightful teachings that I'd long forgotten. Things like, how when given our pocket money, we would rush off and buy holy cards depicting portraits of Jesus and Mary, or any of the myriad of saints. This little childhood ritual would be scoffed at now, but they allowed us hours of harmless fun, trying to imagine what life was like in the Holy Land.

The girl with the most holy cards had a special status and was deferred to by all. The ultimate status symbol in 1959, though, was the iridescent statue of our Lady of Fatima. She sat on our bedside lockers and shone through the wee hours of the morning, protecting us from 'goblins in the garden and things that go bump in the night.'

Scottish Ian, a large, fun-loving party animal, usually organized the evening's revelry. We generally heard Ian before we saw him, his booming voice declaring the venue for that night's gathering where he'd hold court. He insisted on wearing the Medieval garb of a pilgrim: robes and a very big sloppy hat with crosses dangling from it. Ian had recently lost his father to cancer, so his exuberance covered a lot of grief and sadness. Ian and I buddied up on the festive occasions (almost nightly). We shared the ability to drink an immoderate amount of *vino tinto*, having decided that moderation is for monks. He was at least thirty years younger than I, but we also shared very black humour, his coming from being a Scot, mine from a lifetime of working in hospitals.

Nici from New Zealand never seemed phased by the ordinary obstacles which had the rest of us pulling our hair out. Laid back like the Australians but without the larrikin factor, Kiwis are mostly loved wherever they go in the world. She became the undeclared mother/organizer of the group, and could always be relied upon to be sane and balanced. Whenever I asked her what she was up to, she replied, 'Herding cats!' with a look of exasperation on her face.

Between Nici and Ian, our nights became the highlight of the day. New people joined and other companions left, some to make deadlines for work or other commitments at home. Many pulled out because they'd sustained an injury from the excessive walking.

The conversation didn't vary much. One might expect deep and meaningful philosophical exchanges, but the usual banter centered mainly on our feet. The usual greeting was, 'How are your feet holding out?' And we often-heard such things as: 'My new shoes are killing me;' 'I can now brag about fourteen blisters;' 'Should I prick my blisters?' And, 'Where does one find a pair of sandals?'

Sometimes we ventured into discussions deep enough to take our minds off the pain in our feet and the seemingly endless road, but that was usually after a few glasses of *vino tinto* with the evening meal. The further we walked together, the more others joined our group and the more intimate we became. The level of trust we developed was as excessive as all the other aspects of this trip.

The next morning I set out to explore Leon. The walls of the original Roman fortress, built by the Roman 7th Legion around 29 B.C., still stand in the heart of the city, and history oozes out of every corner. The cathedral, Santa Maria de

Leon—also known as Pulchra Leonina, meaning The Leonese Beauty—is one of the more significant in Europe. Unlike most Gothic cathedrals that took hundreds of years to build, it took only sixty years, starting in 1255 when the population of Leon was only 5000 persons. The building is now almost a thousand years old, and it stands in stark contrast to the hot, noisy, dusty streets of the city—protecting the sacred from the profane.

I entered through the heavy wooden doors and stepped into a cool interior with a calming and sacred atmosphere. Everything slowed down. I found myself walking slowly and quietly, as if trying to fade into the background while allowing the tranquility of the ambiance to absorb me.

For those with 'eyes to see,' Templar/Masonic symbols inundate the walls and ceilings, hidden amongst layers of gothic and catholic decorations. I'm fortunate in that members of my family have been active in the Masonic Lodge for hundreds of years, so I'm familiar with the symbolism. The builders of the cathedrals were operative Masons. They wrote their secrets of ancient wisdom in stone so it would remain incorruptible. This arcane knowledge has been handed down through the centuries.

The 4th century cleric St Augustine believed that significant numbers were linked to divinity. By the 12th century, operative Masons used the circle square and equilateral pyramid to underscore their brilliant engineering. The twin pillars or towers, always facing west, and the black and white chequered floor, a symbol of the duality, of good and evil, are obvious signs of their influence. These symbols are commonplace in most Gothic Cathedrals.

Victor Hugo who wrote *The Hunchback of Notre Dame* said: 'From remotest antiquity, the human race has employed architecture as its chief means of writing … Sometimes an entrance, a font or even an entire church presents a symbolic meaning wholly foreign to religion, or even hostile to the church. … Only the initiated can decipher these mysterious books.'

I really needed more than one afternoon to study and observe the sacred history of humankind, written and preserved in stone, but I had to press on and hopefully complete my journey. I've cherished and read books all my life, but I never thought I'd spend a hot afternoon in Spain reading a sacred book in stone. My neck was stiff from craning, and when I left the cathedral, my eyes and body struggled to adjust to the sudden burst of heat, noise, crowds and bright light. I felt tempted to return to the hallowed, calm space now behind me.

The history and culture of the ancient city wasn't all that overwhelmed me. The masseur who delivered my long-awaited massage made something normally commonplace into an outstanding event. His family had lived in Leon for eons and had all undertaken the pilgrimage. Being a devout Catholic, this man—aged in his late 50's—prayed over me, then proceeded to heal my poor worn-out body. I felt a profound release of pent up energy, a very moving experience, summoned by emotion. Instead of being reduced to tears, I was elevated to tears. He described the robust health of my aged body as a small miracle! I described the healing effect he had on my aged body as a *big* miracle!

On the practical side, he advised me on how to walk long distances without damaging my legs. If one walks too slowly, he told me, then the front of the legs suffer. Walk too fast and the back of the knees, calves and Achilles tendons get sore. I took his advice and completed another 300 kilometres easily and injury free. To this day I remain grateful for the advice that man gave me, though I don't even know his name. Things like names, age, race and gender faded into insignificance as our common cause eclipsed all else.

Shaggy friends

False modesty

Nice coincidence

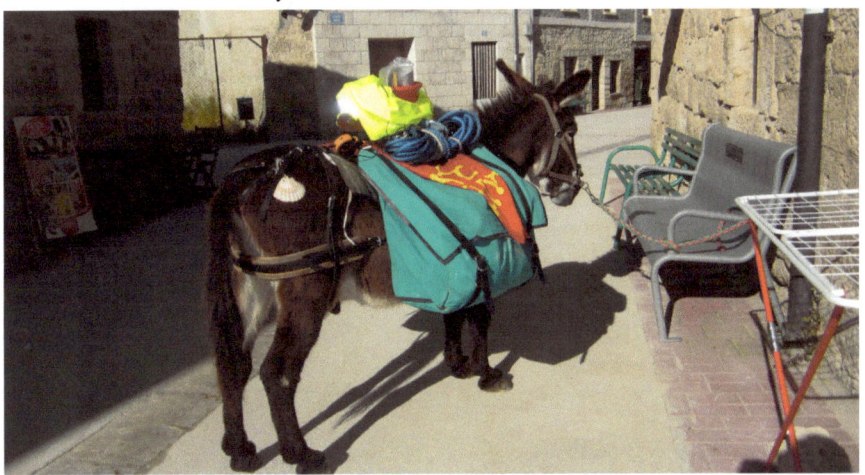
Beasts walking

15. Daily Departures Into the Realm of Shells & Arrows

'I could see every pebble on the path, every blade of grass, by that splendid moon.' Emily Brontë.

I've always chosen to rise early in the morning, usually before sunrise in the first light and regardless of where I find myself in this world. Early mornings ooze sensuality and heighten the senses. The aromas are pronounced, and the light is always unpredictable and ethereally soft. Even the most vivid crimson or golden sunrise has a silkiness to its light. The early morning mist hovering over the landscape diffuses the edges of any harsh manmade objects, and when it ascends, a congregation of songbirds fills the sky with their aria. I love to see the dew undisturbed on the spider's webs and flower petals.

Those who rise early have to move quietly and gently so as not to disturb those who remain in bed. Gradually they develop a sense of ownership and privilege, begrudging anyone who trespasses on their trance. This describes most mornings in the countryside of The Camino. Early morning departures from the large cities are very different but just as splendid.

To have a good getaway early on a dark morning, the prior evening's preparation had to be an exercise in precision—the sort of precision that would put NASA to shame. I arranged all my clothes, water, medication and small amounts of food in the exact same way every night so I could manage by feel in a space half the size of a regular single bed at home.

My departures were sluggish, to say the least. To sustain my life, I had to draw blood to test my blood-glucose levels, give myself two injections of different insulins and take oral medication. Numerous daily dressings had to be applied to my feet, numbering up to twelve at one stage. All this, I did in the dark with a head lamp, trying not to disturb anyone. Once I'd completed that, the rest of the day was a breeze.

I remember walking out from the old city of Leon very early on a Sunday morning, searching for the usual 'shells and arrows' to guide me. A new moon hung in the still-dark sky above the cathedral. The city was deserted after a Saturday night of revelry, the only sounds being the rhythmic tapping of my trekking poles. It had rained, and the orange street lamps gave the wet surfaces a golden hue that contrasted with the black cobblestones. The occasional stray cat shot across my path, and I took a lot of wrong turns. I found it all a little unnerving, and that familiar hollow feeling of being lost arose in my stomach. Eventually, dawn rose, and as I walked thru the long avenues of ancient pollarded trees, more pilgrims joined me.

The Spanish locals' lack of entrepreneurial drive surprised me, given that the GFC was at its peak and impacted severely on Spain. Thousands of pilgrims departed their accommodation early, and it seemed incredible that there were no food or coffee outlets open until around 10 am. The opportunity to make money was there for the taking. Germans generally ran the rare outlets that were open.

The usual way to pick a nationality is by appearances, accent or clothing. However, on the Camino, it was possible to pick the nationalities in the dark by the approach they took to departing the albergues.

First up and away were the Japanese—their discipline and refinement made them stand out from the crowd. Not bothering with anything to eat, they slipped away in the dark, like an ethereal feather melting into the dark without a sound. Sometimes I wondered if they sustained themselves on air alone.

The Germans came a close second. Always in charge of themselves and their circumstances, these *Übermenschen*—superhuman people—clomped around in their heavy boots and strode into the new brisk dawn powered by bread, cheese and sausages.

The French rose early but spent hours consuming an enormous breakfast while huddled around in their little groups, not bothering to connect with anyone else. The Spanish and Italians were the noisiest and least organized—talking fast and loud took priority over eating, but only just! The last to leave were usually the Aussies and Brits, a lot of us nursing hangovers into the already torrid morning.

None of this should've surprised me; I'd just never seen the differences so graphically portrayed, and yet, no hint of nationalism ever surfaced—ever! The hardships provided us with an empowering feeling of connectedness with other pilgrims, with the ruined castles of old dreams, and with those who went before and those who will follow. The landscape informed us every minute of every day, activating a different kind of awareness.

By this time I'd perfected the art of walking with trekking poles. I'd never used these extraordinary poles before, but they were necessary to accommodate walking on my fractured foot.

The support of a pole allows the body to overextend and deliver a kick off from the back foot, a lot like cross-country skiing. It entailed much use of the upper body, literally like swimming. Often I felt as if I were flying down the big white, dusty road surrounded by endless rolling plains of purple lavender, red poppies and golden canola—not a tree in sight. Walking had become effortless.

Traveling, as we were, we forgot the trivial politics we'd left at home, except for those with pointing index fingers. You know the ones! Summoned by emotion or fuelled by the fires of excess *vino tinto*, they fell into the tiresome tendency to lecture everyone from their morally superior pulpits. Feminism did raise its head in Estella, the only place in Spain where women were allowed to fight bulls. The younger girls in our group went to check out the bullfight and then, sickened by the needless cruelty to both bulls and horses, decided to leave that pursuit out of their agenda. No one really mourned the rare event of humans being gored or injured.

This section of the route was particularly beautiful: rolling treeless plains with fields of flowers, crops and pasture, not unlike outback Australia after a wet season. The Anzacs who use the red poppies as their flower were never far from my mind.

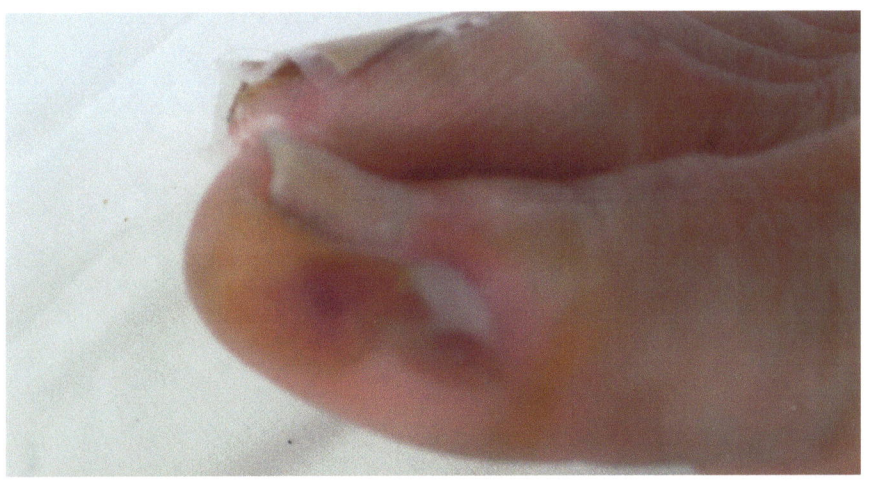
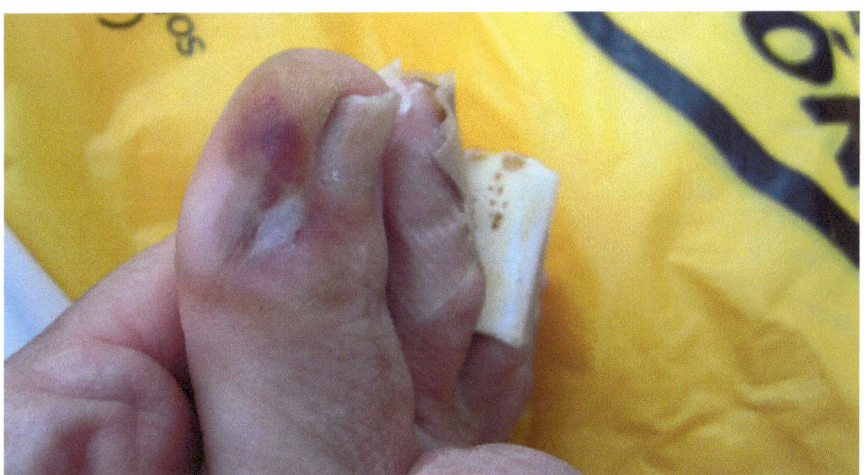

Angry foot, Daily Dressings

Ancient well

The angel from japan

Contentment

Camino Comfort

Dormitory

16. Hospital da Orbigo

'I know I have the body of a weak and feeble woman, but I have the heart and stomach of a king.' Queen Elizabeth I

Rumour spread through our group about a medieval fair happening in a small village called Hospital da Orbigo. Renate and I decided to stop over night in this village to savor the spectacle. We were never disappointed by anything that came our way, and in this case, the fair satiated all expectations, even those we didn't hold.

Our accommodation that night was one of the most delightful places where we'd been lucky enough to find a bed. Centuries old, lots of wooden paneling, thick stone walls and a garden overflowing with herbs, flowers and fragrances. Local art depicting the landscape and cultural life of the surrounding area covered the walls. In true monastic style, the dining area was furnished with long narrow tables and rough-hewn benches made of heavy wood—not that anyone used them, as the evening turned out.

To top it all, I was reunited with Maddy and her new travelling companion, Kay. Because I'd taken the bus for a few sections on the Catalan route, I'd walked in front of her for a few days, but my longer stopovers allowed her to catch up. I hadn't intended to join these two, but it was wonderful to see Maddy again. We had so many stories to share. Their tales of amazing distances covered put us all to shame. She even ended up on the bunk above me in the albergue, and we chatted till late.

In the morning they took off into the ascending sun, dust rising behind them. I waited till that settled before I set out at snails' pace, dodging the thousands of real snails crossing the path from right to left.

This village had staged a jousting festival since the 11th century when it was a Knights Templar stronghold. Spain has these jousting festivals all over the country. They're a celebration of national culture—music, dance, food and the militaristic arts—similar to the Highland Games one finds in Scotland. The air was heavy with the smells of horses, dogs, meat cooking over BBQ's, and the fragrances of freshly harvested vegetables and flowers. The entire village was set out like a medieval market with trestle tables overflowing with local produce, including cheese wheels the size of car wheels—some were so sharp we had to run to find something to put in our mouths to put out the fire!

Medieval tents displayed falcons, eagles and other birds of prey. Some perched on their masters' gauntlets and gloves as they paraded around the food stalls in their Knights Templar or Knights of Malta uniforms, their little sons dressed the same—the tradition is for father to hand on his skills to his son.

The jousting was the highlight of the day, a display of excellent horsemanship and courage. When it started, we noticed, amongst the grown men, a slight figure holding his own with the bigger and more experienced men. We held our breaths when, time after time, he came thundering down the race on his charger, managing to dislodge riders twice his size. The high-impact knocks often threw the rider from his horse, even leaving some concussed on the ground.

We found out later when *she* removed her helmet that her family consisted of only girls, so her father had instructed her in the skills of medieval warfare. She was much loved by the local crowd and astounded the travellers.

After the arena closed, we moved across to an enormous communal barbeque, where seemingly tons of meat were grilled on gigantic steel hot plates. I couldn't remember ever eating that much meat in one sitting, despite growing up on a cattle station in Australia. At home we were at least encouraged to force down the boiled cabbage, carrots and potatoes.

The beer gushed like water as the night rocked on into the dawn. I remember being fully intoxicated with the atmosphere, music, dancing, beer and camaraderie. Another special day. Can they keep coming? I wondered. However, I was disappointed the next day to hear that the young heroine was really a hero! That her story was only a rumour, a Chinese whisper. There was much dispute about this within the group I was traveling with. I didn't stay around long enough to find out the truth. Suffice it to say, regardless of gender, that person held us spellbound for many an hour.

The journey, like good wine, just got better as the days moved on. The first few weeks, because of my illness, were ones of pain, despair and gruelling endurance, but my body had, at last, become used to the mileage. Now the journey was one of joy, friendship, surprise and constant delights to be ravenously consumed.

Centuries of unbroken tradition

Jousting (image from Shutterstock)

Medieval festival

Templar Hospital

Templar Kitchen   Templar Monks

Templar Hostel

17. Ponferrada

'The knight's bones are dust—his soul is with the saints I trust.'
Samuel Taylor Coleridge.

It might be obvious by now that I carry a penchant for all things Knights Templar. Growing up in a strongly Masonic family exposed me, at an early age, to the trappings of 'the Lodge'—I knew, despite what lay people told me, that the Masons didn't ride goats around the temple! Dad, my uncles, cousins and forebears had all practiced Free Masonry, some rising to the status of Master Masons. Our predecessors came from The Orkneys, North East Scotland and Northern Ireland, all strongholds of The Lodge. Often, out of curiosity, I opened Dad's regalia cases, and I can still remember the smell of the soft, white kid-leather apron and how tender it felt in my hands. Sacred symbols adorned it, not in a garish way but with stunning balance and symmetry. The regalia was exquisitely beautiful and well crafted. I was never allowed to ask questions, being both a woman and a child, so when I got older, I studied everything I could find on the history of the Knights Templar. I remain convinced that there's a direct connection between the Templars and the Freemasons, although I'm aware that this idea is considered unorthodox amongst some masons.

On this journey, I saw an overwhelming number of reminders of the Templars' influence on the lives of pilgrims. Unlike now, when Freemasonry is an anathema to the Catholic church, in medieval times they were the military arm of the church, their main role being to protect pilgrims and hold off the armies of Islam.

The most renowned of the Templar fortresses was the castle in Ponferrada. Those of us who pursued this interest waited patiently to arrive at this destination. For me, it turned out to be a day of complete frustration, wonder and crisis.

The day at Ponferrada started in a village only a few hours away. I woke to find myself infested with bed bugs! Shock. Horror. I'd heard that this was a common occurrence for travellers in Europe but had no inkling of just how devastating these things can be. They live in the cracks and folds of mattresses and bed linen, and the only way to get rid of them is to wash *everything* in very hot water. No pesticide will kill them.

In order to have access to a proper laundry, I'd planned to stay at a commercial hotel or B & B, but they were all booked out. So on arrival at the albergue run by the local council—which resembled Gulag 6—I asked for the use of a laundry and a supply of hot water. They gave me a plastic washing tub with a serious leak and told me to boil the kettle on the stove top. I then proceeded to wash all my clothes, pack and belongings in this small leaky tub in the kitchen where people were trying to prepare food. Then I had to walk across a paddock to hang them out on a piece of wire—the word 'primitive' doesn't get close to describing the facilities. The whole process took about two hours. These wretched parasites also hit a fellow pilgrim, Tanja, but she was in a worse state as she had a severe allergic reaction to them. Her face swelled up and pustules formed all over her body. Since we often sought advice in the pharmacias, we became known as the 'Pharmacia Fairies.'

I checked into my bed—a bunk in a basement without any windows that accommodated approximately fifty double bunks. The top bunks sat very close to the ceiling where exposed plumbing ran. Every time the toilet flushed, it made so much noise that the person on the top bunk couldn't get any sleep.

The washing facilities in these council albergues were more than minimilist; they were outside the bounds of acceptability. The shower facilities were works of horror. The shower heads came out of a wall directly opposite the toilet pedestals and so close that you could have a shower whilst relieving yourself. Worse, it was all unisex. Any false or genuine modesty quickly got washed away. Even something as simple as hook on the wall for our clothes hadn't been thought of. Everyone clamoured over each other, too exhausted to complain.

Having completed my 'chore,' I then rushed out to visit the Ponferrada Templar Castle. It was stunning—magnificent, sad and haunting at the same time. Although the inside of the castle had been almost entirely gutted, the external walls stood untouched by the passage of time. I stood spellbound by the feeling of actually standing on the same ground as the legendary knights that spilled out of the pages of Sir Walter Scott's books. My imagination ran wild, visualising the bustling crowds, the superb Arabian horses, the sun glinting on the armor, and the sounds of shouting men, horses neighing and dogs barking above the general din of the markets. I spent hours trying to go back in time, to smell, hear and feel what it would've been like in the peak of its glory.

The mission statement of the Templars, a monastic military organization, was to protect and care for pilgrims across Europe and the Holy Land, and they maintained this service for over

200 years. The path of the Camino follows the line where the Christian armies held up against the Saracens; anywhere south of it was occupied. For this reason, semi-ruined Templar hospitals, churches, chapels, cathedrals and castles lined the path.

Jerusalem and Palestine had been Christian for 300 years before the advance of Islam. The various crusades attempted to take back what was once theirs, but the quest failed after much bloodshed and loss of life. As bloody and horrible as they were, the crusades inadvertently contributed much to Western civilisation. The crusaders liaised with Muslims to learn Astronomy, Architecture, Medicine, Commerce and Law, and the Templars brought this learning back to Europe. This liaison was the turning point for Western civilisation, and few of us are aware of how critical that turning was. The scientific knowledge was instrumental in bringing Europe out of the dark ages. The Templars were instrumental in holding back the Saracen armies and eventually driving them out of Spain. The irony is that the Catholic Church and the French King eventually spelled their demise.

Fearing the power and wealth accumulated by the Templars, the Church and Phillipe IV of France conspired to bring about their demise by mounting accusations of heresy. Many were executed, and others went underground in Scotland to emerge as the Freemasons—a story that is far too involved to go into in this book.

I left that historic site with more questions than answers.

After we left Ponferrada, the landscape became very hilly for a few days, necessitating some serious climbs. We climbed to the highest peak on the journey—1504 metres—on a cool and misty day. As I mentioned before, religious symbols appear in every nook and cranny on the Camino—usually beautiful works of art, even if a little over done—and on this summit, we discovered an enormous cross called Cruz de Ferro, (Iron Cross). A significant landmark on the Camino, built in the early 11th century, the Iron Cross looked as it sounds—harsh, brutal and unyielding.

Christianity didn't adopt the symbol of the cross until the 4th Century, when Constantine became emperor of Rome, freeing the Christians from persecution and banning crucifixion. Before that the cross manifested in varying shapes in Egypt and India. The Egyptian *ankh*—a cross crowned by a ring—represents life and death. In ancient symbolism, the horizontal means death and the vertical means life, so the cross brings the conjunction of two worlds, integrating opposites: vertical and horizontal; human and celestial; feminine and masculine; ying and yang.

Pilgrims place a small stone or object at the base of the Cruz de Ferro, a symbol of leaving their burdens behind or maybe just asking for a blessing. Most leave a small stone or pebble, but the theme has many variations. I saw old boots, names painted on stones, faces painted on stones, pictures of loved ones, crutches, spectacles, a horse's bridle, old love letters, and drinking vessels of all shapes and sizes. Each object symbolized something meaningful to those who placed them there. Some say that the rock you leave should signify proportionally to your sins. I had no idea how I'd get a massive boulder to the summit! I chose to leave a bag of lolly snakes, because for the last thirty years of my life I've had them by my side to elevate my blood sugar levels when they're low. Though a banal object, they're the most important thing I have—literally life savers. Humans tend to look for the sacred in mundane things; I think I took that concept to its limits with that gesture.

Battle Slot   Eternal Vigilance

Ponferrada Castle   Templar Banner

18. Galica in all her Glory

'Far over misty mountains cold.' J.R.R. Tolkien, The Hobbit.

In Galicia the landscape, food and architecture all changed, and it came as a huge relief after the scorching vistas. The land is green and lush, the mist ever present, and moss and lichen cover the trees, rocks and buildings. I felt as if I'd landed in Ireland or Scotland, especially because, due to a strong Celtic connection, it's not unusual to hear bagpipes playing.

Fresh seafood is the staple food, and everyone loves the *pulpo a feira* (boiled octopus with garlic and paprika). It sounds awful but is ever so tasty.

My fellow pilgrims and I were lightening up both physically and mentally, walking briskly, as we knew we had not much farther to go. Much to my delight, we walked though varied topography—even hills and mountains!

After leaving O'Cebreio with its Celtic round stone huts with thatched roofs, I spent the night in a hostel run by Buddhists in the town of Ruitelan. Not what you'd expect on a Catholic pilgrimage! I've spent a lot of time in Buddhist monasteries and retreat centres, struggling with, but admiring, their superb belief system. These places were always Spartan, but very clean and well run. When I checked in, the hostelier was not convinced that I'd walked so far and he felt that if I had, I shouldn't have! It wasn't the first or last time I was told to slow down. From that point on, he referred to me as 'The Road Runner.' Whenever he saw me, he made the Road Runner's well-known squeaks, 'beep, beep.' Clearly I couldn't afford to take offense in this place! Our host lectured everyone, saying that we were *all* walking too fast. His words reminded us that we'd not entirely thrown off the trappings of modern Western civilisation. That night we had a superb communal vegetarian meal—very Buddhist—followed by beers in the pub across the road—very Australian! Another ecumenical experience.

The next day the wind blew the mists away in the hills and woods, but it remained in the valleys, and though I couldn't see far in the misty atmosphere, the sounds of running water, animals, and birds came alive in a seductive symphony. I became entirely immersed into the lush landscape, kept verdant with almost-continuous gentle rain. The trail appeared as if covered in a vivid-green velvet, and alongside it ran streams of crystal-clear water. The numerous small bridges with gentle curves—mainly of Roman origin— spoke of a lasting design that has weathered the ages. I walked this entire day on my own, at a very slow pace trying to absorb the splendour of these primordial beech forests: every twisted limb; every bright-red fungus; the ferns and the time-worn rock fences.

When approaching Samos, I thought I'd taken a wrong turn, a seriously wrong turn, and had ended up in either Inverness or the County Down. Young men in kilts played bagpipes; shops sold haggis and Guinness, and the souvenir shops wouldn't look out of place in the Royal Mile in Edinburgh. And all this sat against a background of swirling mountain mist.

I arrived at lunch time, so I sat down to a warm bowl of hearty bean soup with Nici. We both had Celtic origins and so felt very comfortable with our surroundings. After a cold wet morning, the bean soup acquired extra significance. We sat there together, not saying much, like two people who had known each other for a very long time.

At the end of the day, a Japanese gentleman joined me. He told me he worked as an architect, designing aged care centres in Japan. I also discovered later that he loved to sketch with pencil. While I took photos, he used a time-honored way of recording beauty. I found him sitting in windows, on walls or leaning against bridges, drawing his surroundings. It was so quaint. The only other person I know that does this is my son Dan who also happens to be an architect! Dan drew Venice, a place he described as 'loving as much as one loves a woman.' Very passionate people, these architects. I became separated from him, as often happens on the Camino, but we ran into each other on the last day in the milling crowd in Santiago. We embraced, congratulated each other, then went our separate ways never to cross paths again.

In one of the earthy, bleak little villages in Galicia, I experienced human behaviour that was both remarkable and amusing. After sharing a communal meal with a group of English women and getting quite friendly with them, we went to have a shower. One of the women pulled me aside putting her finger to her lips, indicating secret women's business. She seemed quietly distressed, her face blushing with discomfort. I expected the worst and, having just met, wondered why she wanted to include me in her private life. Then all was revealed:

'I've got the bed bugs,' she whispered, 'but I don't want to tell the others in the group. ... The shame of it.'

The poor thing! The chance of hiding bed bugs from your fellow travellers would be at best difficult. I took her aside and explained the process of ridding oneself of them. She went into melt down. I also said the bed bugs can be picked up in five-star hotels and that there's absolutely no shame in it.

At the end of this bizarre evening, I found that the only bunk left for me was the top bunk. Not normally a problem, but the man below me had some sort of assisted breathing device, maybe a CPAP machine, and the noise was horrendous. I couldn't imagine carrying that heavy machine hundreds of kilometres on a pilgrimage!

The next morning almost all the people from that dorm were early leavers. We beat a sullen retreat!

I never saw that group of English women again.

Murals in Samos Benedictine Monastery

Religious Mural

Renate's high tech raincoat

Samos Benedictine Monastery

The Verdant Path

Medieval Pharmacy

Galician Grain Silo

19. Sarria

'Wilting flowers do not cause suffering; it is the unrealistic desire that flowers not wilt that causes suffering.' Thich Nhat Hanh.

Though the journey had started badly for me and brought a lot of loneliness, by about halfway through, it had changed from misery to pleasure. By the time we reached Sarria, our group had swollen to anything from six to twelve, depending on the pace set and the needs of some to stay longer in certain places. Sarria was famous for two things: octopus and religious processions. Renate and I supped magnificently on *polbo a feira*, (a dish made of octopus), washed down with a bottle of *Laxas*, a white wine.

The religious procession held the following Sunday was the epitome of Catholicism. Days before the event, the local community came forth to line the streets leading to the cathedral with flowers. Petals formed images of the Virgin Mary and other saintly figures in meticulous, colorful and delicate art work. On Sunday morning, accompanied by discordant brass bands and drums, the procession, led by a priest and church elders, deliberately walked through this charming creation, destroying days of work.

The mature-age women following the priest had faces I found frightening to behold. Their stern countenance confused me; I thought this was a day of celebration. I stood in the pressing crowd, holding my breath with anticipation. A collective groan came from the foreigners who watched the deliberate destruction of the flower art in astonishment.

I understood the significance of the congregation's actions, though. Although prior to this I'd only seen it manifest in Eastern society. Destroying the street art was a way of demonstrating the impermanence of all things and the transient nature of the world. A similar ceremony is held in the Himalayan Buddhist tradition; there, a beautiful sand mandala, a physical representation of life, created over several days, is destroyed in a few seconds. A harsh lesson on the brevity of life and matter.

In Sarria the crowd was so pious that I almost felt unworthy of being there. Even our fiercely secular group became absorbed by what they witnessed. I found myself almost envious of the people's complete and unshakeable faith and reverence, thinking how it would give them a feeling of standing on solid ground from birth to death. I felt like an undeserving supplicant.

Serious Beleif

Religious Procession

Kilometers of Devotion

All fresh flowers

20. Monte de Guzo

'Travelling it leaves you speechless, then turns you into a story teller.' Ibn Battuta.

Tanja, a sweet young girl from Germany, Yolanda from Madrid, Stefan from Sweden, Marianna from Brazil, Mona and Patsy, patchwork quilters from Texas, and Charles from California joined our group of Ian, the Scottish jester, Kiwi Nici, Irish Mary, Renate and Dennis, a Kiwi marathon runner. Others came and went, but in the last week, this core group had become a well-bonded band of travellers. We walked together, ate together, drank together and generally shared everything, all with copious amounts of humour. Our ages ranged from eighteen to sixty-eight, but this was never an issue; we were just kindred souls sharing what was probably the most intense and best part of the journey.

Listening to their life stories fascinated me. No one held back, and the tales ranged from silly to serious: failed marriages, successful careers, feral children, pets, cooking recipes, religious beliefs, travel experiences, childhood traumas, teenage fantasies, medical ailments and so on. I had never experienced this level of honesty and lack of inhibition in such a disparate group of people. The Camino had cast a spell on us all.

The pilgrims who'd merged in from the other offshoots, mainly from Madrid and Portugal, crowded the track in the last section of the journey. On the very last day, however, walking into Santiago, I chose to walk apart from the others to savour the exquisite surroundings and reflect on the past seven weeks.

It was another misty day, full of a brooding, soft-green light. Amazingly, Australian Eucalypt trees stood in large groves on both sides of the track, along with the debris of eons of pilgrims. Staffs and worn-out shoes lay amongst memorial crosses draped in religious paraphernalia in memory of those who'd died before getting to Santiago. None of this could be seen as rubbish as all were placed deliberately and symbolized a significant event in someone's life.

To my surprise, I walked the last two hours entirely by myself—something unheard of on this section. At first I thought I must've taken a wrong turn, but the signs demonstrated that I was on the right path. I felt so lucky, even blest, so I walked on in a blissful trance, surrounded by a soft-green, radiant light. The silence and solitude in this lush forest was delectable. Along both sides of the path stood shoulder-height pillars. They may have originally been used as markers for pilgrims, but now thick-green moss and lichen entirely covered them. From a distance, seen through the mist, they took on an almost a brooding human form. They gave an eerie feeling to the atmosphere, and because I was there on my own, added an edge of slight fear—invisible forces were afoot. I had an astonishing feeling that something mysterious reflected back to me from my surroundings, and I sensed my mind reaching into the limits of credibility.

You can imagine the shock when suddenly an airbus flew over me at a very low level! It jolted me out of my medieval reverie and thrust me crudely into the 21st century. I was on the outskirts of Santiago and had brushed up against the international airport.

At the next stop, I joined our group to walk into Santiago where the journey ended; this was an experience to be shared. The narrow, cobbled streets with very little wheeled traffic led us into the large square where we looked up at the gloriously imposing Santiago cathedral with its famous spires—dark grey/green from 800 years of witnessing ecstatic pilgrims and an almost constant light rainfall. Bagpipes and drums played in the ancient stone archway—more evidence of the Celtic origins of this place. The mood was festive, and the joy in the air palpable. We all hugged, kissed and congratulated each other.

Ian, Our Event Planner

Our Special Pastors

Supplications, Memories & Gratitude

The Final Day

Two Very Miserable Women

21. Santiago: The Pilgrims' Mass

'How happy is that guardian angel who accompanies a soul to holy mass.' St. John Marie Vianney.

We arrived in Santiago with the things we'd collected—experiences, relationships, maturity, humility—and not sparing a thought for the things we'd discarded—hard opinions, clothes, books, cameras, fatty tissue, arrogance, and ignorance. We'd collected each other, a motley crew of folk who somehow or other had arrived at the same time and place, enjoyed each other's company and grown from shared experiences.

The climax of this pilgrimage is the pilgrims' mass in the Santiago Cathedral, the burial site of St. John. I was the only Catholic—though lapsed—in our group; some were Protestants and others assertively secular, but they were all excited—how bizarre is that?

When the time came, we climbed the stairs, entered into the vast sacred space, and took our places in the pews as close to the altar as we could get. During the mass, a nun sang hymns with the most sublime voice any of us had heard. Trying to describe her face, I come up with words like plain, utilitarian, austere, stark and stern—not a skerrick of emotion. As a child in a Catholic convent, I remember those sorts of nuns, and I would've been terrified of her, but when she started to sing, the hairs stood up on the back of our necks. It was truly transcendent. When she finished singing, she just snapped her hymn book shut, shoved it under her arm in a very unceremonious style, turned on her heels and strode out of the cathedral, a day's work done. We were astounded that the voice of an angel could emerge from someone with such a bleak persona. Little did she know of the power of her voice to alter people's souls and consciousness. I'd started this journey seven weeks prior, standing in awe of the human voice in Montserrat, and it seemed fitting to finish on the same note—literally.

The ceremony finished off with the ritual of the Botafumeiro, one of the most awe-inspiring religious events in the world. The Botafumeiro is a giant thurible—a metal censer suspended from chains—which has been used since the 12th century to clean the air with smoking incense when pilgrims arrive at the completion of their long journey. Weighing in at sixty-three kilos, it takes eight men hauling on ropes to hoist it to the ceiling and swing it across the top of the congregation. We were all simultaneously reduced to tears and elevated to ecstasy.

I realized that my whole life I had dismissed differences and paradoxes. I'd chosen to take on all the available belief systems—how naive. But some belief systems and religions are so stagnant that, locked into medieval dogma and animistic fables, they find it impossible to escape their inertia.

However, I took comfort in the alignment of Christian and Buddhist teachings. Although they differ greatly in their message, the compassionate heart is the core strength of both. Buddhism is basically a system of ethics unparalleled in its perfection. Buddhism rejects hard dogma and blind faith, asking instead for adherents to continually question everything until the last breath. Christianity, on the other hand, adheres to strict dogma and asks for blind faith, so they are strange bedfellows. Although the Christian faith took some disastrously wrong turns, it has left a legacy to Western civilization which has yet to be surpassed. Every day on this journey demonstrated the beauty of European music, arts, literature, architecture and altruism. I came away with a lot more respect for Christian European culture than I had when I started.

After the mass our little group stood around outside unusually quiet and somewhat sheepish about surrendering their emotions to a medieval religious rite. Sensitive to the struggle taking place before me, I tried to render it less harrowing with the best tool I have—humour. So, acting the clown as usual, what else could I state but, 'Say what you like about the Catholics, but they put on a bloody good show.'

This may seem irreverent to some, but it came from a place of sincerity and love. After that we relaxed into laughter and high spirits. I feel that the power of appropriate humour remains unappreciated and underutilized.

Finally we have made it

The Pilgrim's last supper

Santiago Cathedral (Image from Shutterstock)

22. Passport to Nowhere

'Bizarre travel plans are dancing lessons from God.' Kurt Vonnegut.

The last day finally arrived. A lot of pilgrims went on to Finistere as the final leg in their journey. This small town on the coast represented the edge of the world to medieval travelers. I'd had enough of walking by then, though, and chose to enjoy my time exploring every corner of the old city.

I felt that all the hard work was behind me and it was appropriate to relax. Little did I realize what lay in store for me with Ryan Air and bed bugs. I had a flight booked from Santiago to Barcelona, departing at 6 am on Sunday. It was common knowledge that if one didn't check in online the previous day, there would be a substantial financial penalty, somewhere in the region of seventy euros. I found the only internet café in town and proceeded to check in, paying three euros a half hour for the privilege. Ryan Air's website and check-in process was shamefully hard to negotiate. I was asked to enter the nationality of my passport, but they provided no option to type it in, just a scroll-down showing all the countries Ryan Air serviced. To my amazement and despair, Australia wasn't listed! No one spoke

English; the place was about to close, and I was in full panic mode. I decided to select Austria and hope that the good folk at the airport wouldn't notice—a desperate move, but the only option available to me at that moment.

That evening with everyone in a celebratory mood, we gathered to enjoy our last communal meal with its usual generous Spanish servings washed down with *vino tinto*. Addresses were swapped, photos taken and a few tears shed, both happy and sad. It was then that I felt stings on my hands. When I examined them, I saw blood blisters the size of green peas springing up all over my hands, fingers, arms, ankles and neck. When they came into contact with anything, they ruptured and bled! My roommate, Tanja, sat beside me experiencing the same outbreak of bed bugs. We thought we'd thrown them off a week ago and were both devastated. We quickly returned to our lodgings and washed everything in boiling hot water.

The following day I got up at three in the morning to catch the bus to the airport. The Saturday night boisterous celebrations were still in full flight, with young drunken people roaming all over the place. At first I felt intimidated, but when they came up and spoke to me at the bus shelter, I realized that they were all just out to have a good time and were amazed to find an old woman from Australia waiting for a bus at that hour of the night. Our language barrier prevented me from explaining the situation, but they appeared both impressed and amazed.

On arrival at the airport, I was almost shaking with apprehension, not knowing if they'd see the discrepancies with my check-in, but I'd conjured up a plan of sorts. Sure enough, when I presented at the baggage check-in, the lady behind the counter picked up on it, so I activated my plan. I acted like someone who was intellectually challenged, stating that I couldn't comprehend the check-in procedure. She went from being very aggressive to very caring and escorted me over to another desk, where they decided that I was not a threat to security and waved me through! My immediate relief was overwhelming, and my anxiety vanished.

When I eventually put my very-much-reduced frame into the airline seat, I said a heartfelt prayer thanking God for delivering me from all the calamities of a wonderful journey back to my loved ones and beautiful mountain home.

Jim Whittaker, the first American to summit Everest, once said, 'If you're not living on the edge, you're taking up too much space.' I concluded that I hadn't taken up too much space for those last seven weeks. I'd danced on the head of a pin ...

A Diabetic Perspective

For those readers who are confused between diabetes type 1 and diabetes type 2, I'll explain the differences. Type 1 is insulin dependent and type 2 is controlled with diet and oral medication. I have type 1 diabetes.

This disease has you permanently living in a state of duality. Spiritual teachings from both East and West instruct on how to deal and recognize duality and also how to strive to reach a nondual state on a higher plane—a place that eludes me and most other people I know—but in this case, the duality is enforced by your physical state. Your blood sugar levels fly from high to low or low to high at any given time. One is constantly looking for food with either no carbohydrate or excess carbohydrate/sugar. Exercise goes from being essential to dangerous (with hypoglycemia). Moods alter drastically, depending on the unpredictable highs and lows, and that makes it difficult to maintain human relationships.

Diabetics have to be grateful for the discovery of insulin, as it allows us to survive, but aside from chemotherapy, it has to be one of the most dangerous drugs currently used to treat a disease. In my case, it only requires one unit of insulin, which is barely visible to the naked eye, to kill me. Luckily there are only a few us who are this brittle.

This disease demands constant vigilance, twenty-four hours a day, seven days a week, fifty-two weeks a year. There are great variances in the spectrum, and I've been told that I have one of the most difficult types. They call it 'brittle' diabetes. Some people need up to eighty units of insulin a day, some less than ten. This is dictated by BMI, (Body Mass Index, a measure of height against weight), energy output, carbohydrate intake, stress levels, random viruses, fluctuating hormonal levels in women and all sorts of vagaries that are too numerous to mention. Because I've always been slightly built and very active, my insulin requirements have always remained minimal. After thirty years of living with this affliction, I must admit I'm starting to tire of it. I visualize this disease as one of those ugly gargoyles that sit on gothic cathedrals, ready to pounce the minute you take the eye off the ball. Ironically, I saw many of them on this journey, perched on roof corners, ugly and leering.

I've found myself close to unconsciousness with very low blood sugar levels in the most random of places, but usually it happens in the lounge room in the safety of my own home. At these times the most benign place on the planet for me is transformed into a metabolic war zone simply because I've misjudged a dose of insulin by one unit. For many years, I was lucky enough to have a Border Collie dog who would alert me through the night to hypoglycaemic episodes. Penny from Heaven. Literally. Unfortunately for me she now resides in Heaven, and her departure has left me flying by the seat of my pants.

Because I refuse to be contained by this disease or the medication used to treat it, I've found myself having such episodes in the most bizarre places, ones you wouldn't choose to die in—the top of a mountain, the back seat of a taxi, and in front of a vending machines bearing an 'out of order' sign in the wee hours of the morning. On that occasion, I was tempted to grab a brick and smash the glass door that separated me from the lifesaving high carbohydrate junk food.

Once it happened while I waited in line in a shop. The person in front argued for a long time about some trivial exchange while sweat ran down either side of my spine, my hands shook and my peripheral vision faded, but hard-wired to be polite and wait my turn, I said nothing. I've discovered that hard-wired polite behavior can be deadly. I've always embraced delayed gratification, so before I grab some sugary delight to shove into my mouth, I'll hang up the washing or do something equally trivial and unimportant. This is because by the time it gets to this stage, the blood sugar is so low that the brain's ability to make rational decisions is so compromised that the brain reverts to learned behavior. For me, delayed gratification, which should be a virtue is lethal.

In the second week of this journey, I reduced my slow-acting insulin from twenty units to ten units per day, and by the fourth week I'd reduced it to two units per day. After the second week, I didn't use the fast-acting insulin at all. This means that I'd reduced all my insulin by ninety-eight percent and still experienced hypos on a regular basis. I started off carrying bags of snake lollies, but I needed so many that the weight of them forced me to change to Kit Kats that were light. I remember arriving at one destination towards the end of the journey, only to count eighteen empty packets of Kit Kats. And that was in one day of walking. The girls I travelled with were jealous because despite that intake, I was still losing a lot of weight. I lost ten kilos in seven weeks! To this day I don't understand how all of this played out, because no one in the medical profession appears to be interested to look into it. Suffice it to say that I survived and lived to tell the tale.

Many query my motives for staying the course and persevering to the end. My explanation is that I have observed the way that diabetes affects people differently. It seems to take your personality and drive it into the deepest part of the soul. Idiosyncrasies, both positive and negative aspects, become more apparent. If you're easy going and relaxed, that quality seems to become more pronounced. If you're driven and ambitious, that characteristic takes over. If one is feckless, the end is nigh. With me, stubbornness and bloody-mindedness came to the surface, along with a cast-iron will—a very dangerous combination, especially as the Jesuits declared that the only thing that burns in hell is willpower!

I'd never advise anyone against walking the Camino because they're diabetic, but I'd suggest they take an easier path and an easier pace, and not to adopt such a cavalier approach to any journey.

Epilogue

People quite often ask if there is anything 'not to like' about the Camino, and I always reply, 'Lots.' This often comes as a surprise to many, but it's my truth. It may not be the same for everyone. Some would say, 'Nothing to like,' and others would say, 'Everything to like.'

Some days I found myself hating it. Long, boring, hot stretches of deserts; ugly industrial perimeters of cities; nasty hostellers; the list is endless. A lot of trekkers look for pristine wilderness, beautiful landscapes and crystal brooks tumbling through unspoiled forests. Those things appear toward the end of the road in Galicia, but if they expect them all the way, they'll be sorely disappointed. This is a journey of the mind, soul, history, culture and personal relationships—it's pretty thin on eye candy.

The landscape I traversed was mostly hot, flat and dry, but as we approached the northern areas it became mountainous, cool and misty. The dreaded Meseta, in Spain's heartland, was a completely flat plateau with virtually no shade trees and nothing to distract the mind from the unbearable tedium. A lot of people chose to take a bus across this section, but the walking of the Meseta was worth the discomfort. The land supported more agricultural than pastoral activities with fields of purple lavender, yellow canola and green barley juxtaposed against the endless white ribbon of the road.

The area we walked through also included moderately sized cities with all the amenities and chaos of similar places all over the world and small villages, delightful in their somnolence and their quaint dwellings with well-tended gardens. The horizon always featured deserted forts or castles, evidence of centuries of conflict. Often we were lucky to spend the night in one of these.

My journey left me with enduring impressions of that time and place: the landscape, the people, the food, the architecture and the religion.

I've enjoyed the companionship of many Spanish folk throughout my life time, but to live amongst them on a daily basis was a very different experience. The first thing I noticed was a complete absence of apology, for anything! They are fiercely proud and unapologetic of their culture, history, language and religion. The *mea culpas* that many politically correct politicians from the West roll out seemed to be missing. I acknowledge that there's an appropriate place to ask forgiveness for past wrongs, but the whole thing seems to have lost all relevance as it's been overdone—like dolphins and debutantes. The other feature of their daily life was an unbridled passion about anything and everything. At first I found it exhausting, but then I started to readjust my thinking and began to actually enjoy it. I never had to double guess how anyone felt—a refreshing change from the reserved natures of Anglo-Saxon Celts.

Their generosity was immense. No such thing as half-filled glasses, bottles or plates; there was always plenty to go around. Often I felt frustrated by their lack of drive and attention to detail, but in the final analysis, I found this overshadowed by their endearing finer points. Some of their virtues could be described as quaint or old fashioned, but I found them refreshing and almost defiant in a world that has gone belly up to political correctness.

The food—the single most important thing to most of the travellers—was always fresh, plentiful and very affordable. In the smaller villages, it was common to eat fresh produce pulled from the garden that day and bread, meat and cheeses sourced locally. Every town or village had its own style of bread, but the one thing they had in common was that they cooked bread fresh every day—since they used no preservatives it went rock hard after twenty-four hours. In Galicia, in the north of Spain, it was common to sup on seafood. I've never been that fond of octopus, but they had a special way of cooking it that rendered it tender and delicious. I never experienced a wine that wasn't first class despite it being inexpensive and even free with some pilgrims' menus.

Spain is a veritable smorgasbord of architecture, ranging from the pre-roman ruins to Gaudi and everything in between. Living in a young country like Australia, I'm starved of concrete evidence of history, so I found being treated to so much on a daily basis sumptuous. The most puzzling buildings were the Gothic cathedrals built in cities with very small populations. They must have been built by people driven by religious zeal and a belief in sacred geometry. Those times had a special energy to them.

I believe that architecture is one of the most significant activities of mankind, and very often overlooked, but it is one of the forces that guides our movements and consciousness. The impact of Catholicism—the causal agency in this entire project—on architecture is writ large with every step on the Camino. It surrounds one continually. At first it's a little confronting for those unfamiliar with its excesses, but little by little, it almost seeps into one's pores, penetrating the psychological armour of the most irredeemably secular. Unlike the sparse, controlled, minimalist spaces of the Protestant reformers, the Catholics let rip with irrepressible, profuse opulence, a riot of colour, music and form.

Processions, led by stern-faced clergy and ardent women. Rituals where the choirs lift the audience out of their ordinary lives. One cannot help but be captivated by the fervour. Despite the journey being overtly Catholic, occasionally Hindu centers and Buddhist retreats and hostels offered superb hospitality and spiritual guidance if needed.

I received an excellent education in Catholic convents—not that I recognized it at the time. Most of us were 'kids from the bush'; all we wanted to do was run free. We hated the strict routines and hard discipline. However, we soon came to love the religious rituals, feast days and the rhythm of the monastic life. French and Irish nuns introduced us to the classics, the ideas of the Renaissance, the Enlightenment and the Reformation—the pillars of Western civilisation. Most of us abandoned our spiritual practices when we left boarding school. We emerged into the sixties revolutionary hippie era, deluged with options when it came to belief systems. Jimi Hendrix didn't sit easily with the sung vespers! It's not hard to guess which we abandoned.

Since then a lot of us have grown up and started to appreciate the Catholic faith and its heritage, an appreciation cemented in me by walking through those great Gothic cathedrals, listening to sacred music and viewing the works of art that hung from ancient walls. Working in hospices with members of the clergy opened my eyes to their contribution, but my Camino experience confirmed what I have subconsciously known for years.

Many have questioned why I didn't quit when the struggle and medical problems became overwhelming. Apart from being stubborn and determined, it's because I viewed all that happened through the prism of a medieval pilgrim. He or she would've been astounded at how easy it was for us. The sometimes harsh conditions made me thankful for the abundance of our modern lives. An abundance that sadly, our contemporary society does neither recognize nor appreciate. We had copious amounts of transport and medical support, no marauding thieves, no leprosy, and no shortage of food and water—ever.

I have been fortunate enough to travel far and wide, good places and bad, pristine wilderness and congested urban areas, but his seven-week journey is one of the most profound experiences I've ever had. If I was given the opportunity to do it again, I wouldn't hesitate.

A Note From the Author

Did you enjoy my book?

If so, I would be very grateful if you could write a review and publish it at your point of purchase. Your review, even a brief one, will help other readers to decide whether or not they'll enjoy my work.

Do you want to be notified of new releases?

If so, please sign up to the AIA Publishing email list. You'll find the sign-up button on the right-hand side under the photo at www.aiapublishing.com. Of course, your information will never be shared, and the publisher won't inundate you with emails, just let you know of new releases.

Acknowledgements

I would like to thank my family for putting up with the never ending requests for help with the wretched computer.

Also:
Tahlia Newland, mentor, advisor, editor and publisher.
Ken Methold, my advisor in all matters literary.
John Griffin, 'fixer upperer of my bad grammar.'
Brian and Chris, my very patient computer teachers at the Kiama Library.
Brother Peter Codd for answering questions about the Catholic Church articles of faith and deeper theology.

www.ingramcontent.com/pod-product-compliance
Lightning Source LLC
Chambersburg PA
CBHW042229090526
44587CB00001B/2